Freehand
Drawing

for architects and interior designers

W. W. Norton & Company

New York • London

Book design by Josep Guasch
Composition by Ken Gross
Production Manager: Leeann Graham

Library of Congress Cataloging-in-Publication Data

Delgado Yanes, Magali.
        [Dibujo a mano alzada para arquitectos. English]
        Freehand drawing for architects / [texts, illustrations and exercises by Magali
Delgado Yanes and Ernest Redondo Dominguez; translated by Maria Fleming Alvarez].
                p. cm.
        Includes bibliographical references and index.
        ISBN 0-393-73179-0 (pbk).
        1. Architectural drawing – Technique. 2. Freehand technical sketching –
Technique. I. Redondo Dominguez, Ernest. II. Title

NA2708.D4513 2005
720'.28'4—dc.22   2004061073

W. W. Norton & Company, Inc., 500 Fifth Avenue, New York, N.Y. 10110
www.wwnorton.com
W. W. Norton & Company Ltd., Castle House, 75/76 Wells St., London W1T 3QT
0 9 8 7 6 5 4 3 2

Freehand
Drawing

for architects and interior designers

Translated by Maria Fleming Alvarez

Con-
tents

Introduction

An architect refines ideas and develops plans using the basic tools of drawing. With these tools, the broad, suggestive strokes on the blank page give shape to the ideas. At the end of this process, the final plans, with which the architect gives instructions, lead to the construction of the building.

In this book, the fruit of ample experience in the teaching of architectural drawing, a mix of technical and artistic drawing, we occupy ourselves exclusively with what we consider the most essential and indispensable skill: freehand drawing. We try to be pragmatic, offering simple but rigorous strategies and methods. We introduce the fundamental concepts of drawing and geometry, of architectural space and form.

Anyone who wants to develop a deep understanding of architecture must master all of its graphic components, beginning with the sketch, a drawing accomplished by a rapid freehand movement with a conventional instrument (pencil, felt-tip pen, etc.), which allows for precision and a fine line. The objective is to give geometric definition to any shape by applying a series of graphic conventions and appropriate systems of representation. These allow the architect to survey and analyze any architectural construction from different points of view, as well as determine accurate measurements for any plan. The architect must then learn to create a drawing for the plans. Drawings, freehand or otherwise, done with an agile and expressive hand, with a variety of instruments (softer pencils, graphite sticks, pen, etc.) are either synthetic and schematic, sticking more to an idea, or more precise in the definition of the contours and in the treatment of shadow and texture. They are proportional drawings that suggest volume, texture, and light as it interacts

"The drawing is a language, a science, a means of expression, a means of transmission of thought. By virtue of its enduring power as the image of an object, the drawing can become a document which contains all of the elements necessary to evoke the drawn object in its absence."

Le Corbusier

About the Authors

Magali Delgado Yanes earned a degree in architecture from the Universidad Politécnica de Cataluña, specializing in construction. A licensed architect, she teaches at the university and at the Escuela Técnica Superior de Arquitectura in Barcelona in a variety of graphic disciplines, both conventional and computer based.

Ernest Redondo Domínguez holds a doctorate in architecture with high honors from the Universidad Politécnica de Cataluña in planning, urbanism, and history. He also teaches at the Escuela Técnica Superior de Arquitectura, where he was director of the Department of Architectural Graphic Expression I from 1996 to 2002.

with spaces not yet constructed, suggesting in this way the final appearance of the structure.

Finally, the architect must possess some understanding of truly artistic drawing, beginning with the sketch, quickly done and highly expressive and free, capturing the sensations and proportions of greatest interest in the structure. Or perhaps a fragment of a building, in a particular milieu, showing the urban or natural environment of the structure. The architect must create these sketches with the greatest economy of means and intentionality, so that they remain fixed in the mind. Thus the architect learns architecture with a rich repertoire of experience that, ultimately, will redound to the quality of the projects.

With all this the reader will then be able to tackle, with sufficient knowledge, the creation of plans to scale, while advancing in the training and the use of color in architecture. Nowadays, the architect can acquire these skills not only through traditional means but also by computer, but this distinction lies beyond the scope and aim of this text.

We hope that study of this book will satisfy the curiosity of those who desire to learn something new and further their understanding of drawing and architecture. We hope that the book will enrich the sensibility and expand the graphic vocabulary of readers, and that with practice, they will acquire a fluency that contributes to more fluid communication between the mind and the gesture, between oneself and others.

NOTE TO READERS

Measurements in this book are given in metric format followed by imperial approximations in parentheses; dimensions in the drawings are metric. To convert meters to feet, multiply by 3.2808; to convert centimeters to inches, multiply by .3937.

materials, tools, and Graphic resources

"THE APPRENTICESHIP, THE ACQUISITION OF THE CAPACITY TO LEARN ARCHITECTURE ALWAYS CONTINUES TO BE BASED, IN MY OPINION, ON LEARNING TO SEE, TO UNDERSTAND, AND TO EXPLAIN."

Alvaro Siza, Essay on drawing and construction.

the.Materials.
instruments

ÁLVARO SIZA.
IDEA SKETCH IN FOUNTAIN PEN

and accessories.

Drawing is equivalent to leaving a mark or a line

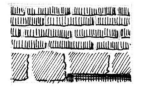

on a base with an instrument, thereby evoking an idea. In this relationship, the graphic media must complement one another. Therefore, knowledge of their characteristics and compatibility is essential to avoid ruining our work. The evolution of different graphic materials has been constant throughout history, from the humble piece of burnt wood to the most sophisticated indelible marker, from papyrus to acetate. With these tools, many artists have managed to express the most varied sentiments. Nowadays, a wide selection of tools of very varied characteristics exists for drawing. All can be useful, but for architectural concepts like light, texture, contour, edge, etc., nothing surpasses the subtlety and nuance of charcoal on Ingres paper, the delicate lines of the graphite pencil on a simple sheet of paper, or the flexible line of a fountain pen on a glossy base.

Graphite. Stroke and intent

We prize graphite for its agility, flexibility, comfort, and ease of correction, and because it creates both the finest lines and the most extensive shading through adjustments to the hardness, the thickness, and the sharpness of the lead. It is probably the most versatile and sensitive medium that exists for drawing.

QUALITY AND HARDNESS OF THE PENCIL

The lead, a mix of graphite (a variety of carbon) and clay, is encased in wood, usually cedar, or held within a mechanical pencil. The higher the carbon content, the higher the quality of the lead. The quality directly impacts the final drawing; a good pencil responds more truly and with greater sensitivity to the intent and pressure of the hand. The clay that is added in the production process increases the hardness of the lead. A standard nomenclature indicates the grade, starting from the middle (HB); H denotes the hardness and the B the softness. The range of hardness is very broad, extending from 9H to 8B, but we will select the leads that best fit our graphic needs, namely those that fall between 3H and 3B.

In general, the degree of hardness is indicated at the end of the pencil.

QUALITY OF LINE

As the hardness of the lead increases, the line becomes more fine and more gray, which is appropriate for drawings based primarily on lines, like the sketch. The more technical the drawing, the finer and more continuous the line should be because it requires greater clarity and precision. The lines for cross-hatching, definition of edges, contour, finishing, and auxiliary lines all fall within this group, with the appropriate hardness ranging between 3H, 2H, H, and HB. But if one wants a more expressive line, for example, for lines that define the border between light and shadow, lines for texture or general shading, the best choices are 3B, 2B, B, and HB; the softer the lead, the more sensitive, intense, and opaque the resulting line.

Two of the mechanical pencils in common use.

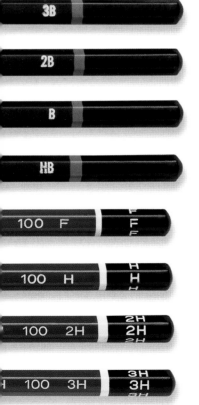

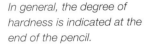

Correct selection of the thickness and hardness of the leads is the first step to successful drawing.

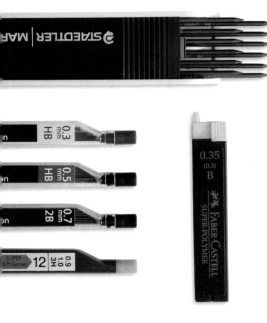

THICKNESS OF THE LEADS

The most common leads are 2 mm thick. Calibrated leads also exist, with a standard diameter ranging from .3 to 5 mm. Their use is increasingly common because they do not require sharpening.

The hierarchy of lines, generally referred to as the linear value, is achieved with different combinations of hardness and thickness. Together with the paper, these components provide the interplay that allows us to choose the appropriate graphic tools. On many occasions, a drawing may require varied grades of hardness and thickness. All this is intended to orient the reader, since each individual has particular tastes and preferences, frequently based on personal and accumulated experience.

Graphite leads are produced in a variety of grades of thickness and hardness, which makes the mechanical pencil the most widely used tool.

Pencil dimensioned sketch of a fragment of the floor plan and section from the plans for the chapel on Mt. Rokko, Kobe, Japan, by Tadao Ando.

Mechanical pencils with the most appropriate thicknesses and their corresponding lines.

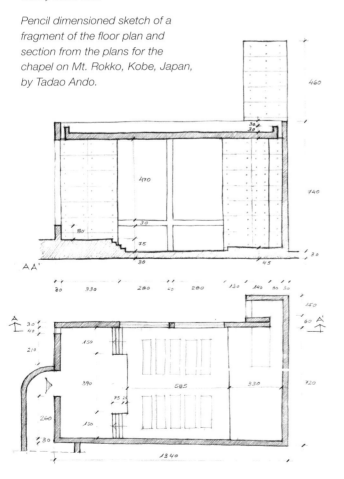

Pencil sketch of the facade from the plans for the Hoffman House, East Hampton, New York, by Richard Meier. The different line values have been achieved with leads of different hardness and thickness.

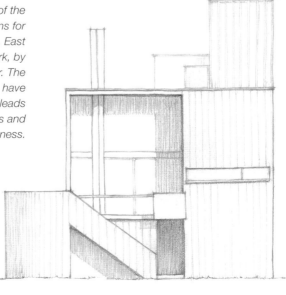

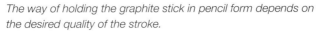

The way of holding the graphite stick in pencil form depends on the desired quality of the stroke.

GRAPHITE STICKS

Graphite also comes in the form of square or rectangular sticks, or in hexagonal pencils with different grades of hardness. These sticks are appropriate for heavy and intense strokes with variable thicknesses.

The principal characteristic of the polygonal bars is that they are not sharpened. They are intended for use on the face or on the vertex of a cross section. Thus, the placement on the paper and the wearing of the edges that occurs in drawing allow different types and thicknesses of stroke, whose intensity will depend on the chosen hardness.

The pencil-shaped stick produces marks of different thicknesses both from wear and from the sharpness of its point.

Graphite sticks, both pencil-shaped and rectangular, provide a great complement to the pencil.

Graphite stick with rectangular section. Corresponding stroke and proper grip.

Sketch with graphite stick of a section from the plans (not built) for the Guardiola House, Puerto de Santa Maria, Spain, by Peter Eisenman. The medium used allows large shaded areas to be created easily.

Using the black colored pencil and the charcoal pencil properly requires more practice and experience than the graphite pencil.

ALTERNATIVES TO GRAPHITE

The charcoal pencil is composed of a slender bar of compressed charcoal encased in wood. The generic name for these pencils is charcoal, and different companies produce them with different grades of hardness. One variation is the carbOthello by Stabilo, a pastel crayon in pencil form that is manufactured in a variety of shades.

The principal use of these pencils is to complete areas where the strokes are invisible except as shading. Because the marks are soft, a slight touch of the finger is sufficient to blend them.

The practical use of charcoal pencils in architectural drawing is limited to faint shadows, light backgrounds, and, because they cover rapidly, large shaded areas. The tonal range of the charcoal pencil is very different from that of graphite, which makes it a good complement.

The black colored pencil is composed of a nucleus of pigment bound with clay encased in wood. Since it produces very black tones, this pencil is used for drawings that require a great deal of contrast.

Drawing in charcoal pencil from the plans (not built) for the Guardiola house, Puerto de Santa Maria, Spain, by Alvaro Siza. The technique permits strong contrasts in the drawing.

Black pencil sketch of the museum-house of the Elsa Peretti Foundation F.P., Sant Martí Vell, Girona, Spain, illustrating the great intensity of the stroke achieved with the black pencil.

The strokes and marks that the charcoal pencil produces are easily blended.

The black pencil is appropriate for very intense strokes.

Ink. Precision and shading

Ink, because it cannot be erased, confers a spontaneous and uninhibited quality when used to draw contours and edges. However, it is a very laborious technique for the representation of shadows or textures, since the basis for their creation is lines or strokes of varying lengths, close together or superimposed.
We begin with some common instruments, not exclusively for drawing.

THE FOUNTAIN PEN

When studies or rapid sketches are needed in unusual locations, such as while traveling or with a third party in a dialogue explaining architecture on an unconventional surface, the fountain pen is the most versatile instrument. First, because as a writing tool it is fairly common to have one on hand. Second, because it combines the majority of the advantages of traditional nibs, while being cleaner and more durable.
The sensitivity of the pen to gesture and to pressure, its flexibility, which makes it capable of generating expressive strokes, and its accessibility make this a very appropriate and useful instrument in architecture.

Fountain pens are very personal, both in the selection of them and in their use.

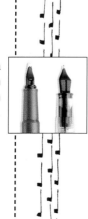

Drawing with a reversed fountain pen produces a much finer line.

Sketch with fountain pen of the historic section of Girona, Spain. The sensitivity of the gesture is very characteristic of drawings with this technique.

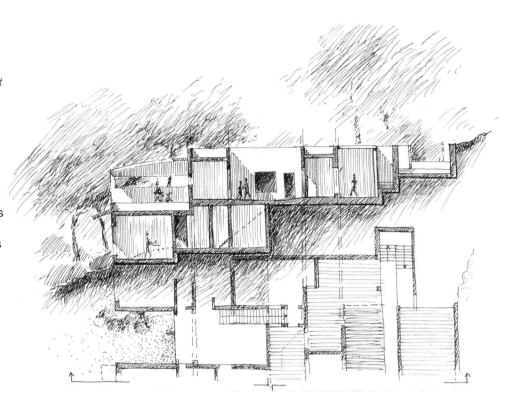

Idea sketch with felt-tip pen showing a section and floor plan from the plans (not yet built) for the Guardiola House, Puerto de Santa Maria, Spain, by Alvaro Siza. In it, large shaded areas created with many lines generate different degrees of darkness.

FELT-TIP PENS

Felt-tip pens offer the same qualities as the fountain pen; however, the line that they produce is not as expressive, thus requiring different combinations of thickness. The recent appearance of felt-tip pens with flexible tips has addressed this problem. Felt-tip pens are available at very reasonable prices and in a variety of thicknesses and tones. We recommend the black-ink models, with fiber or roller tips, especially those with fine and flexible tips. Less necessary are those with medium or thick points. The same technique is used for both felt-tip and fountain pens, since they rely on strokes to create shading and allow for very dark, dense areas that are impossible to erase.

LINE AND CHOICE

If a drawing requires homogeneous, uniform lines, as in the case of the dimensioned sketch, for example, felt-tip pens of different thicknesses or the fountain pen are appropriate. If, on the other hand, a flexible, expressive line is required, as for idea sketches and thumbnail sketches, flexible felt-tip markers and the fountain pen will be the right instruments.

For lines and hatching, the fountain pen and felt-tip pens with the finest points are used. For dotting and other heterogeneous textures, use implements with flexible points.

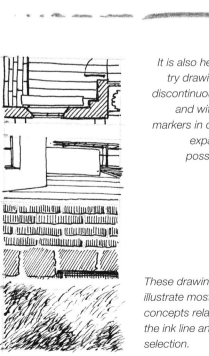

It is also helpful to try drawing with discontinuous lines and with worn markers in order to expand the possibilities.

These drawings illustrate most of the concepts relating to the ink line and its selection.

Paper. A universal support

We will concentrate on the most versatile supports and the most manageable and easy-to-find sizes available, basically the opaque materials.

QUALITY

Paper quality is primarily determined by its weight, that is, its weight in grams per square meter in the metric system and its weight per ream (weight in pounds of 500 sheets of a given size) in the United States. Paper weights range from 80 gsm (50 lb) for writing paper to a maximum of 200 gsm (90 lb) for cardboard or Bristol board. The greater the weight, the thicker the paper and the higher its quality. The selection of a particular paper will depend on the technique that you are going to use.

TYPES

Papers can be translucent or opaque. Among the translucent papers, we may mention parchment or baking paper and vellum, especially appropriate for tracing, but of scant use in freehand drawing except as a complement. Normally, paper should be opaque, since the pencil does not stand out otherwise, and its surface quality should range from a smooth gloss to a medium grain.

A special paper is the tracing or sketching paper, of simple quality and yellowish color, which is very useful for rough drafts.

SKETCHBOOKS

Paper comes not only in loose sheets but also in sketchbooks, in standard or designer sizes. Books are especially useful for sketches of all kinds, as a way of systematically creating a collection of different drawings from a trip or visits to places or buildings of interest.

The range of papers suitable for architectural drawing is somewhat limited compared to that for artistic or color drawing.

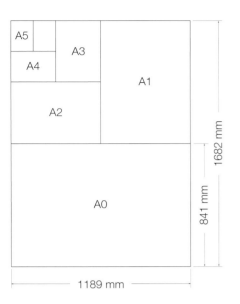

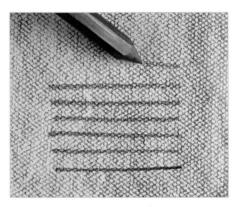

Effects of paper grain on line.

SIZES

Some paper is produced to international (ISO) standards for size. We use ISO A3 and ISO A4; standard American equivalents are 11 by 17 inches and 8½ by 11 inches. In selecting the appropriate size, it is important to keep in mind the proportions that should exist between the dimensions of the subject to be drawn in relation to the paper on which it will be drawn, as well as the ease and comfort of working with a particular size. For instance, it is not the same to draw seated, with a drawing board, as on foot, taking the measurements of a building.

Diagram showing the different ISO formats, from 0 to 5. AO measures 33.1 by 46.8 inches; A1, 23.4 by 33.1 inches; A2, 16.5 by 23.4 inches; A3, 11.7 by 16.5; A4, 8.3 by 11.6 inches; and A5, 5.8 by 8.3 inches.

RESULTING LINE

On a glossy sheet of paper the line is more uniform, smooth, and continuous, which results in a more precise and neat drawing. As the grain or the roughness of the paper increases, the line loses continuity and gains expressiveness; the drawing becomes warmer.

Every visual representation calls for a particular kind of paper. A smooth paper, of fine grain, is appropriate for a dimension sketch, while paper of fine or medium grain is best for idea designs and thumbnail sketches. As for technique, as a general rule, the pencil works better than ink on paper of greater roughness, but here, too, the choice will ultimately depend on personal preferences.

Many types of sketchbook are available.

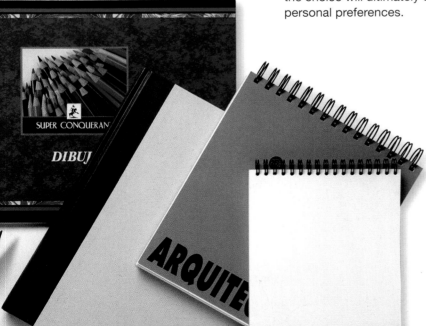

Accessories
and useful complements

A

B

C

Different varieties of erasers: plastic (A), kneaded rubber (B), artgum (C).

the materials described on these pages, while not strictly necessary for sketching, are essential adjuncts for any architectural drawing. As always, we look for maximum simplicity and minimum quantity.

ERASERS

In architectural drawing, unlike artistic drawing, the function of the eraser centers almost exclusively on eliminating errors and unnecessary lines. The eraser's capacity for modifying the quality and the tone of lines and shadings is a minor consideration here.

Among the varieties known for their effectiveness, soft erasers work very well for graphite. They are produced in a classic rectangular shape. More recently, other erasers have appeared on the market, such as the click erasers that hold the eraser in a barrel like that of the mechanical pencil. These allow for very precise erasure, eliminating small parts of the drawing without affecting the surrounding areas. Malleable kneaded rubber erasers are the most appropriate for use with the charcoal pencil.

A circular click eraser, very useful for precise erasure.

Knife with retractable and sectional blades (A) and with fixed blade (B).

SHARPENERS

Sharpeners allow adjustment to the points of different drawing implements, giving you the desired thickness for a given piece of work.

Conical pencil sharpeners are the most commonly used for cedar pencils (with variations in the length of the cone) and mechanical pencils. Some are very elementary, while more sophisticated models collect the waste material. More basic options for sharpening include files and cutting implements like the pocket knife, razor blade, or mat knife.

A

B

Different models of pencil sharpeners.

Rulers help to determine the format measurements of the dimensioned sketch.

RULERS AND SQUARES

Measuring instruments are used in an exceptional way in architectural drawing: they serve as the basic implement in formatting, especially in the creation of the dimensioned sketch. The ruler and the set of square and triangles are particularly important. The ruler is used for sketching and measurement of straight lines, the square and the triangle for producing parallel and perpendicular lines, as well as the principal working angles (30°, 45°, 60°).

MEASURING DEVICES

The dimensioned sketch should reflect the measurements of the architectural elements described. These figures are fundamental data, generally acquired by means of tape measures, which can extend up to 50 m (150 ft) in length.

The electronic tape measure allows an individual to measure by standing at one end of the distance to be measured. The device emits a ray that is projected toward the other end, showing the result on a digital screen.

Squares and triangles are supplementary instruments. They are only used to frame certain elements and measure specific angles in making sketches.

For measuring shorter lengths, flexible metal measuring tapes are essential.

Clips to secure paper to a support.

To measure distances up to 50 m (150 ft), cloth or plastic measuring tapes are used.

Plastic or masking tape is used to affix paper to a drawing board.

the Hand,
the gesture

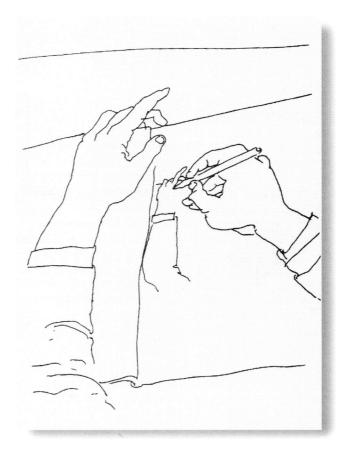

and the observer.

Drawing is observing, analyzing, and representing

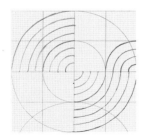

a reality or an idea. And in this process, the mind, the sight, the posture of the observer, the hand, and the gesture form a channel of communication that must be completely in tune with the graphic tool and the medium so that the ideas flow from the brain to the paper.

It is important, then, to understand and become skilled in graphic movements, to overcome the limitations of representing large forms and spaces, such as the difficulty of drawing curves or lines of a certain length. It is also important to learn to look, to retain an image and its proportions.

In architectural drawing all of these factors are complicated by the form of the ideas or concepts, the understanding of which is the objective of other disciplines, but secondary to this one.

In terms of the purely graphic, learning to draw involves a method and an attitude that only with practice and persistence grants us the same fluency and comfort that we experience when writing.

the act of drawing should feel as natural as writing; this means that the hand must hold the pencil (or other drawing implement) without tightening up, without tiring. When we write, we create letters, symbols of very limited extension and variable orientation; when drawing, on the other hand, we create longer lines that flow in a designated direction.

the Gesture and the hand

Natural manner of holding the pencil.

WAYS OF HOLDING THE GRAPHIC TOOL

There are different positions for holding the pencil, the pen, or the marker, depending on the length of the line. The first and most common placement for the hand is only somewhat higher than the normal grip for writing. The index finger and thumb hold the pencil, and the pencil rests on the middle finger, at a slight angle with respect to the apex of the hand. In this position, good lines of about 6 cm (2 1/4 in) in length can be drawn with a slight inclination. These lines tend to be the most natural, precise, and intense. When we draw horizontal or vertical lines of similar extension, we feel obliged to change the angle which the hand forms with the forearm. In the case of curves, the hand resting on the paper acts as a pivot.

Some longer lines require constant adjustments of the hand on the paper; this movement should be accomplished carefully to avoid altering the intensity and direction of the line.

Repositioning of the hand for drawing vertical lines.

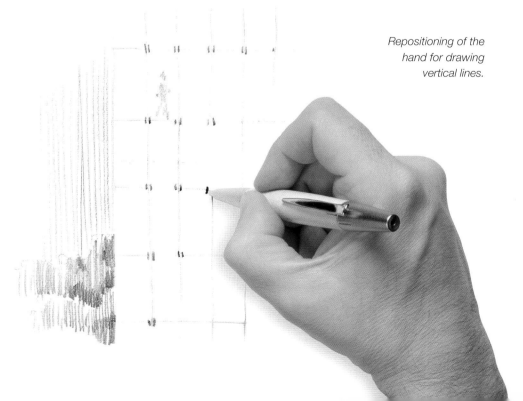

Position of the hand in drawing horizontal and curved lines.

The second way to hold the graphic implement is used to draw formatting or supplementary lines. For these longer lines we must adopt a more relaxed hold, since they require that the hand move over the whole support with complete freedom of motion. Thus, the hand does not rest too firmly on the paper. The same considerations apply for making long horizontal, vertical, or curved lines.

Position of the hand for formatting a dimensioned sketch.

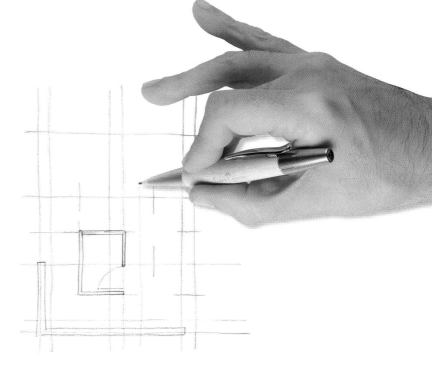

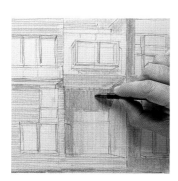
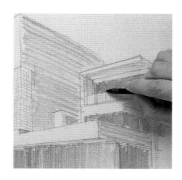

The graphite stick is held in a different way in order to produce closely spaced lines.

The third position for holding the drawing implement is the most relaxed. Here it is held a little higher than in the previous case, and is used for hatching or other repetitive lines that call for little pressure on the paper.

However, if the shading or hatching is defined by contour lines, then the hand should adopt a posture close to the first position, depending on the precision needed. Obviously, the same considerations for the type of line apply here as well. Everyone holds a pencil in the way that feels most comfortable; the key is that the position should not limit the freedom of movement that the drawing demands. These hand positions apply for implements that draw both in a rising and a descending line, such as the pencil and the marker. This is not the case with the fountain pen, whose asymmetrical point only flows in a descending motion and therefore requires a rigid grip.

The characteristics of the pen line influence the manner of holding the implement.

LOOKING IN THE DRAWING OF LINES

The eye should always focus first on the place where the line begins and then shift to the point where the line will end, since the eye guides the stroke. Otherwise, if the eye follows the drawing implement, the orientation wavers and the lines become irregular. With a little practice, the lengths of the line link together consecutively when they are very long, in the same way that the beginning reader learns to look to the next word of a text while still pronouncing the previous one.

For shading the grip should be light, since a repetitive motion is required for the darkest shades. The hand should be able to move loosely, with agility.

The hand and the eye should move together in directing the line.

STRATEGIES

Other strategies are helpful in the case of drawing long formatting lines, both vertical and horizontal. Holding the pencil as high as possible, the palm of the hand and the little finger slide along the edge of the paper, which should be affixed to a rigid support, thus allowing for the creation of long lines as far from the edge as the pencil can reach. Occasionally, a grid can be used as a guide. Sometimes a series of points can mark the trajectory of the line; similarly, small straight lines can indicate the different directions that the line will follow when these are connected. Lastly, it is possible to turn the drawing board until the placement of the line becomes more accessible and comfortable.

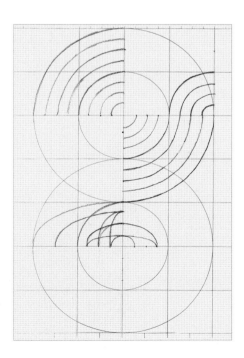

The best way to overcome these challenges is practice with many exercises in executing different kinds of lines.

Position
and body posture

everyone talks about rapid drawings, at most one or two hours in duration, but this does not mean that the posture of the person sketching and observing should not be comfortable and stable. The place must be warm and protected from inclement weather. Preferably, one is seated or stands with points of support so that the paper can be held as firmly as possible. The support, therefore, should be a hard surface, and the sketchbook should have a cover of very rigid cardboard.

Otherwise, or when using loose sheets of paper, it is best to lean on a small board; when on foot, the board is held against the abdomen with the hand that is not used for drawing.

In the case of the dimensioned sketch, this more technically precise drawing incorporates numbers and lettering to show different projections of space. In other words, the dimensioned sketch combines a thoughtful, abstract drawing with the collection of data, obliging you to move around through the space. The ideal posture for producing these drawings is as close as possible to the posture used for writing, raising the eyes from the paper only for visual verification.

When producing a natural perspective study, that is, when drawing an architectural setting from a given point of view, it is important to consider various issues: whether the angle is interesting and whether you will be able to return to the original spot after changing position. Making a mark on the ground with a pencil or with tape facilitates this maneuver. In these drawings, it is important to avoid looking away from the model as much as possible.

It is best to be seated to make a dimensioned sketch.

If it is not possible to sit, at least lean against a support with some part of the body.

Another possible position for greater comfort.

Hands and body should form a solid ensemble. When drawing horizontal and vertical lines it is very helpful to slide the hand along the edge of the drawing board or the rigid cover of the sketchbook.

We frequently are obliged to move around to get a better view; in this case it is helpful to leave a mark at the exact place where we were drawing.

To make a dimensioned sketch, you must be able to move around to take measurements.

It is important to choose a comfortable and protected location.

the Graphic alphabet. Its richness

ANTONIO SANT'ELIA.
INK SKETCH

and complexity.

Architectural drawing is the sum of a

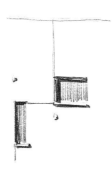

series of strokes, more or less linear, on a page. The line, as an abstract representation of an edge or material limit, is the basis of its alphabet, and the graphic conventions and systems of projection, its grammar.

Our drawing, a mix of the technical and the artistic, carries a greater richness of expression. Therefore, architectural drawing requires more from the line, the texture, and the shading that express the qualities of a material, the surface and volumetric characteristics of the different architectural forms, probing the concepts of shading and tonal values. At times the representation of the setting incorporates entourage: vegetation, furniture, the human figure, etc., in a symbolic and realistic manner. And as a descriptive document, a medium for the transmission of data or instructions, the architectural drawing requires measurements, labels, and the customary annotations. Architectural drawing blends graphic convention and intuitive gesture, rigor, and expressiveness.

line and the Graphic alphabet

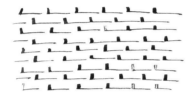

drawing is like writing, with the difference that rather than use letters as graphic signs to form words and convey meaning, in drawing we use lines to describe the formal qualities of objects. This means that the relationship between the location and separation of the lines on the paper should correspond to their relationship in reality. The line is the fundamental element of the graphic alphabet for any designer. In the same way that a written document is more legible and comprehensible if throughout it titles are emphasized with larger print and smaller print is used for footnotes, and proper names and sentences begin with an uppercase letter, in drawing there is an equivalent established graphic hierarchy. The lines, like the letters, must be neat and decisive in order to facilitate reading them.

TYPES OF DRAWING

As with a legal document, a prose text, or a poem, in each one of the three main types of architectural drawing that we address, the dimensioned sketch, the idea sketch, and the thumbnail sketch, nuances and assessments arise with respect to the use of the linear graphic alphabet. We use a variety of lines: continuous lines, either uniform or expressive, are used for layout or to convey edges; discontinuous lines, in dashes or dots, indicate the hidden and projected edges and borders; and discontinuous lines in dashes and dots show the axes of symmetry and composition.

Using more expressive lines, we can describe many kinds of motifs.

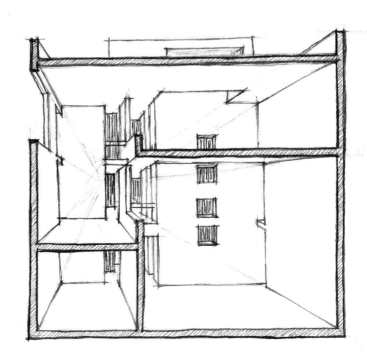

Pencil idea sketch of a section from the plans for the Turegano House, Pozuelo de Alarcon, Spain, by Alberto Campo Baeza. Different continuous lines are used for layout, definition, and outline.

LINEAR VALUE

Regardless of the type of drawing and the lines used to complete it, our objective should be to emphasize the important features, contrasting them against the secondary or anecdotal. Given that we cannot modify the size of the lines, as occurs with letters in writing, either we grant the lines greater or lesser thickness in varying combinations, or we play with the intensity of their tone. The result should be considered as a whole, since the architectural drawing constitutes a unitary document. In the dimensioned sketch, which is a more conventional, regulated representation, the graphic alphabet must be applied with greater rigor, assigning linear values according to the importance of an architectural element. In the idea sketch and the thumbnail sketch, by suggesting the depth of the represented space, its superficial appearance, its lights and shadows, the graphic expression is more pictorial and edges sometimes lose importance in the service of the other values. Again, in architectural drawing it is important to establish a more perceptual hierarchy and unity.

Different lines employed in architectural drawing. By combining these lines, one can produce strokes or shading with lines or points or both to give greater priority to the effect of the whole than to the detail.

Pencil dimensioned sketch of a section from the plans for the Gwathmey House, Amagansett, New York, by Charles Gwathmey. Here the linear values are achieved by varying the thickness and hardness of the leads.

Graphite pencil drawing from the plans for the Volador House, Vienna, Austria, by MVRDV architects. The linear value in idea sketches deals with different concepts than those in the dimensioned sketch.

Shading
through the juxtaposition of lines

In the perception of reality and in its representation, more than contours and edges, of fundamental importance are the tone of an object or its color, its texture and surface quality, the shading that denotes its volume, and the contrast with its surroundings.

These last four aspects are reproduced by means of tonal shading in both drawing and black-and-white painting. In the case of line drawing, the effect of shading is achieved by the juxtaposition and superposition of points and lines, which appear more or less dense and saturated depending on the thickness and hardness of the medium used.

TONALITY

Objects are illuminated by sources of light. This light, in the form of energy, is absorbed, reflected, and transmitted by materials. The light that is not absorbed generates the color that we perceive, chromatic value in a strict sense. This color is systematized by the sum of three values, hue, saturation, and brightness. In this book we concentrate on the achromatic attributes of light, which is to say that we will not talk about color, but rather the tonality of a material, the quantity of black or white in its hue.

We differentiate between the material's own tone and the tone that results from the surrounding environment, which we call the middle tone. By half-closing our eyes, we can perceive the complementary middle tone, whereas we perceive the characteristic tone of the material when we focus only on a given element.

Examples of architectural motifs produced with linear shading and different techniques.

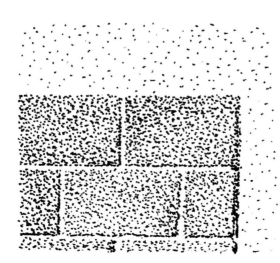

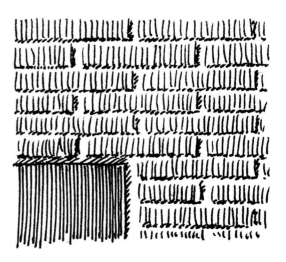

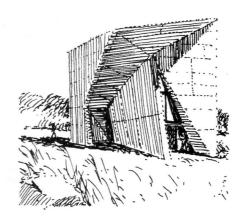

Ink thumbnail sketches from the plans for the chapel in Valleacerón, Spain, by Sol Madrilejos and Juan Carlos Sancho.

SHADING WITH ACCUMULATED LINES

Thanks to the juxtaposition of tones, we appreciate the elements of a scene as areas of contrast, discontinuity, edges, and changes of texture. Depending on the type of representation of these tones, we differentiate between drawings of contour or edges, in which the lines define the borders, and drawings with shading, in which changes in tone define everything. An intermediate representation would use both techniques simultaneously.

In the dimensioned sketch the lines always play a complementary role, defining textures or sections in a uniform way with planes enclosed by edges. In idea and thumbnail sketches the particular tone of surface, its volume, textures, and shadow are represented in a freer way, using gradients and not always edges as a border.

TONAL SCALES

Reality and its representation are different things. The first presents hundreds of tones, whereas with a pencil only a few dozen can be produced. Assuming that the maximum light or absolute white is the tone of the paper (not colored paper) and that absolute black or the absence of light is the densest and darkest tone that can be obtained by saturation of the line, these become the two extremes of the scale. Between them, taking as reference the tonal scales used in photography, eight tones remain to define everything else. Most important, the scale must be measured so that the space between each tone and the next is uniform. Otherwise, more tones will be needed. Therefore, before using a graphic instrument, it is helpful to draw several scales, combining the strategies of shading explained below.

Pencil thumbnail sketch of an urban landscape in Barcelona, Spain, done with linear shading.

Ink thumbnail sketch of the previous urban landscape. Very linear shading with ink should be done with a great deal of control and patience.

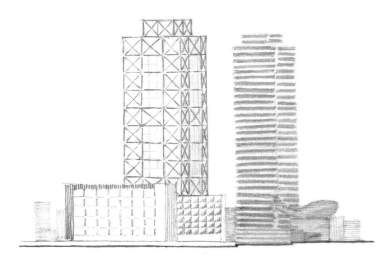
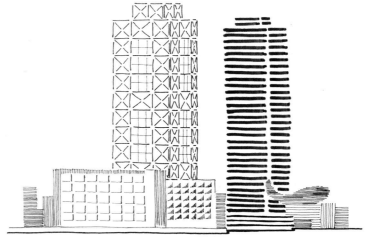

*Tonal scale of shading
done in pencil.*

SHADING TECHNIQUES

In order to achieve the number of tones mentioned, different shading techniques can be used. We will concentrate on the most common ones in architectural drawing.

The simplest shading is directional, and we divide it into two groups: the first is unidirectional, obtained by the juxtaposition of lines of identical value very close together, varying the separation between the lines until, at the normal distance of viewing of a drawing, they are indistinguishable (the concept of blending).

We differentiate between uniform directional shading, whose tone is kept constant, and variable directional shading, whose intensity or tone varies. Variable directional shading allows for decreasing or increasing the hardness of the lead while playing with the pressure of the instrument on the paper. In the case of tools for uniform lines, one must combine diverse thicknesses.

Multidirectional shading is achieved by superposition—that is, by the accumulation of two or more sets of unidirectional shading oriented in different directions. The contrast between the direction of one layer of lines and the next should not be very great, in order to avoid generating an undesired texture.

The third technique for shading is to use stippling, or dots. The tonal scale is obtained by the juxtaposition of the dots or small lines more or less close together, depending on the desired level of darkness.

The fourth technique is heterogeneous shading, or free lines, used to represent elements whose texture is more irregular and characteristic.

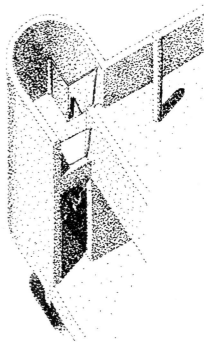

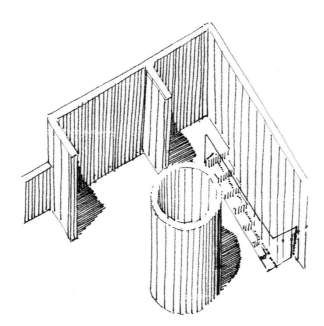

Ink sketches in axonometric perspective. Details from the plans for a single-family home by Richard Meier, created with different shading techniques: from top to bottom, multidirectional, stippled, and unidirectional.

EXPRESSION OF UNIFORMITY AND GRADATION

There are two important tonal expressions: uniform tone, in which a single tone is maintained throughout its extension, and gradient tone, in which a tonal scale is reproduced within a chosen area.

To produce a uniform tone requires practice, since the process of shading with fine-pointed graphic tools over a large area, while easy, can be very laborious because the lines are thin and close together.

In order to obtain gradient tone, the technique is more complex, requiring the juxtaposition of areas of different tones throughout the whole area to be shaded. The transition from one area to another must contain intermediate tones, lightening from the darkest tonal register or darkening from the lightest.

The technique of heterogeneous lines is recommended for its flexibility and rapid execution. A drawback is the difficulty of defining the edges of the shaded area. One solution is to indicate or enclose it by lightly dotting the edges.

From top to bottom, decreasing gradation in ink. From left to right, a uniform tonal register.

Ink idea sketch from the plans (not built) for Danteum, Rome, Italy, by Giuseppe Terragni. Shading describes the space with different degrees of uniformity and gradation.

textures. A specific application for shading

textures represent one application of the techniques of shading in architecture. They explain the surface qualities of a material and indicate its nature. The perception of the texture of a material depends to a large extent on the distance at which it is observed. In this sense, one must differentiate those representations that have a more descriptive character, such as idea and thumbnail sketches, from the more abstract ones, like the dimensioned sketch.

SYMBOLIC REPRESENTATIONS FOR THE DIMENSIONED SKETCH

In the representations of texture, the tonal values of the material are not described, but rather the structure, in a symbolic and simplified manner depending on the scale of the drawing. At a certain distance, one that implies a lesser scale and less detailed drawing, the image is symbolic, not the real appearance of the subject. Although in some disciplines there exist very rigid conventions for representing different materials, this is not the case in architectural drawing.

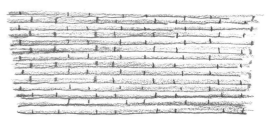

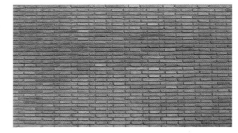

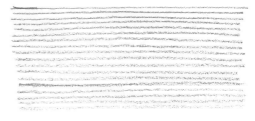

Brick wall at different distances and scales, and its drawn representation.

EXAMPLES OF DIFFERENT APPROACHES

Below are a series of common representations. These can serve as a reference in dealing with other materials. It is important to remember that these graphic indications must complement the lines that define the architectural elements, and they must possess an obviously lower hierarchical standing.

Examples of the representation of different materials and elements.

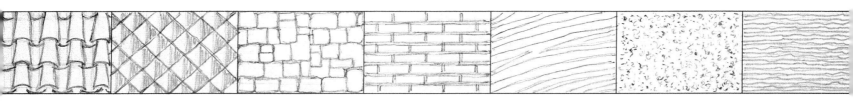

| Roof tile | Ornamental tile | Stone | Brick | Wood | Lawn | Water |

REPRESENTATIONS IN PERSPECTIVE

In perspective drawings the process of abstraction or simplification of the lines in the distance is produced in a continuous manner, passing from very descriptive foregrounds to distant areas in which the texture of the material is barely evident.

The texture is simplified with distance by reinforcing and suggesting the depth and distance of the different surfaces. When the textures in the drawing are combined with shading lines, it is best to use different processes and expressions for each. In the drawings here, the texture of the materials is used to represent a space; observe that the appearance of the materials is described at the same time as the sensation of depth.

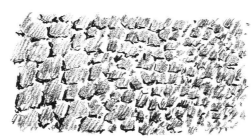

Stone wall in perspective and a representation of it.

These exercises are good practice for different scales of representation. The previous examples of textures can serve as models.

Black-pencil thumbnail sketch of the Noves House of the Elsa Peretti Foundation F.P. in Sant Martí Vell, Spain. The texture of the stone is an essential element in the description of this construction.

Ink idea sketch by Arne Jacobsen. The texture of the brick, created with a series of continuous lines, gives a sense of depth.

a variety of relevant factors influence the perception of reality or the understanding of a representation of reality. Among them stands out the shading of an object, composed of the object's own shadows (shade) that denote its volume and its cast shadows, which show the relationship of the object to others nearby. These shadows, together with the areas of light or highlight, are reproduced by means of tonal shading or hatching. In drawings with linear strokes, the shadows are executed with lines.

Shading.
The perception of light

SIMPLE LIGHT SCHEME
Every scene that we see contains a variety of objects or surfaces illuminated in contrast to their shadows. This phenomenon is called a light scheme, and it is composed of the sources of light, the tone of the materials that delimit the objects and their shadows, and the shadows cast by other objects.

SOURCES OF LIGHT
We can classify the sources of light according to their form and intensity, whether they are environmental or inherent, extensive or localized, directed or focal, omnidirectional, direct, or diffuse. The first source of light, which should be thoroughly understood, is the sun.
The sun is a source of light located in the infinite distance. It emits parallel rays of light and its position with respect to a scene is defined by the direction of its rays, or the solar angle. This angle is composed of two variables, the orientation with respect to north and the degree of elevation.

Charcoal thumbnail sketch of a space from plans for the expansion of the Escuela Técnica Superior de Arquitectura de Barcelona (ETSAB), by Josep Antoni Coderch. Charcoal techniques facilitate the rendering of light in this space.

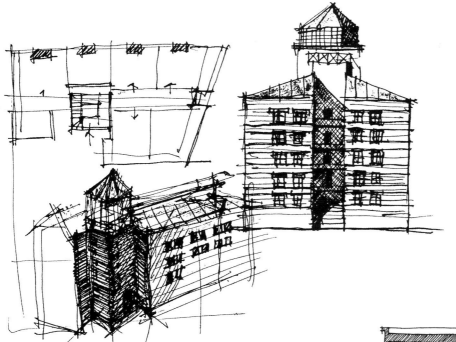

Ink sketches by Aldo Rossi, plan, elevation, and perspective. The shading is achieved with linear strokes.

In architectural drawing, uniform shading is used as much as gradients, depending on the technique used and whether more or less pictorial representation is desired.

Ink dimensioned sketch

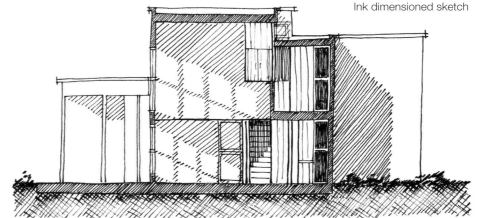

In the dimensioned sketch, solar light should not generate very saturated or dark shadows whose tone or line would hide the nature of surfaces, nor should intensity be lost with distance. In idea and thumbnail sketches solar light becomes a more realistic source of light, more environmental and less uniform. Shadows appear with gradations of intensity depending on distance, fading away depending on the nature of the surfaces where they are cast.

Artificial lights are localized illuminations, of limited surface, which may cast their light over the scene in an omnidirectional or a directed way. Omnidirectional sources of light emanate in every direction, as from a simple lamp. Directional spotlights use baffles or lenses to direct the illumination, which is a concentrated light. When the light source covers a large surface, as in the case of a panel of fluorescent lights or a window, it is considered an extensive source of illumination, and the quality of the illumination is more uniform.

Shadowed sections from plans for the Hoffman House, East Hampton, New York, by Richard Meier. Appropriately drawn lines communicate the exterior light in these drawings.

Pencil dimensioned sketch

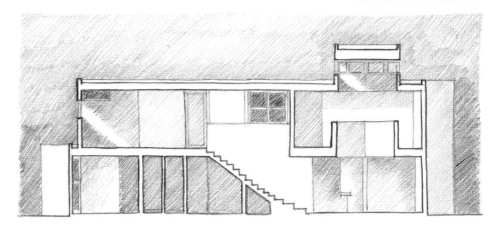

SHADE

A shade is generated when one part of an object or space is exposed to the light and another hidden. The edge or contour defines the border between light and shadow (considered the intersection of the sun's rays tangential to the surface). Shade is an important factor in the perception of the whole object or space, since its absence flattens the forms for lack of depth. In terms of representation, shade corresponds to shadowed areas. The shade is, thus, a veil or darker tone that is superimposed over the tone of the material and, when applicable, over the texture.

CAST SHADOW

Cast shadows occur when an area is hidden from the light source by the shadowed portion of an object or wall that lies in the trajectory of the light source. This type of shadow determines the relationship of a form to the immediate surroundings, and its representation constitutes the counterpoint defining the darkest area. If the cast shadow is projected over a surface of the same material, it will appear darker than the shade originating from that surface. The greater the depth of the surface, the darker the cast shadow.

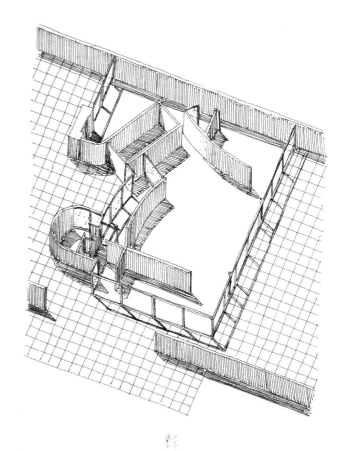

Ink idea sketch from the plans (not built) for the Casa Patio, by Mies van der Rohe. The shadows, cast and otherwise, help to clarify the reading of the volume.

Black-pencil thumb-nail sketch of the Petita House, part of the Elsa Peretti Foundation F.P., in Sant Martí Vell, Spain. The shade on the buildings, together with the shadows cast on the ground, define the scene.

INTERRELATIONSHIP OF OBJECTS

The interrelationship of objects complicates the initial light scheme because the qualities of the reflected light on the surfaces of all the elements in the scene are converted into small sources of light that bounce off or transmit part of their tone onto nearby objects. In this sense, it is easy to understand that in a space covered with mirrors there are no shadows.

GLINTS, HIGHLIGHTS, SHADOWS, AND PENUMBRAS

The introduction of shadows when attempting to represent a space requires the use of a tonal scale, just as shading does. The tone of the observable planes and their representation will vary according to the intensities of the light sources and their orientation. Depending on the degree of exposure to light, different tones are assigned to the features of an object, tones for the shade and tones for the cast shadow.

The two extremes of the achromatic tonal scale are highlights (in this case, the sheen of the paper) at one end and the most intense shadows at the other. Beyond these values would fall, on the light side, glints and, on the shadow side, total darkness, values to avoid since they cannot be reproduced graphically.

Graphite pencil idea sketch from the plans for the Shamberg House, Chappaqua, New York, by Richard Meier. The highlights and glow of the surfaces, in addition to the shadows, are intentional.

atmosphere and surroundings

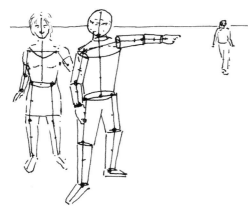

Charcoal thumbnail sketch by Mies van der Rohe.

In architectural drawing, the entourage or incorporation of figures, vehicles, and vegetation in a scene illustrate the use of the different spaces and communicate their human scale and their integration into the proposed natural or artificial environment of the building. Their form varies, from the most symbolic and schematic employed in the dimensioned sketch, to the most realistic in the idea and thumbnail sketch. We will concentrate on the dimensioned sketch, since the other forms of representation tend to be more pictorial and expressive, requiring greater experience. However, we consider some mastery of simplified representation to be fundamental, and its application universal and adaptable to architectural drawing, so long as its presence does not undermine the intentions and values of the drawing and of the architectural model.

THE HUMAN FIGURE

The skeleton is drawn first, giving coherence to the different parts of the body and the possible attitudes or postures. It is important, thus, to understand the standard proportions for the parts of the body. We can simplify the task by using a canon or rule, with the measurement of the head as the basis for defining the measurements of the most important parts of the body. Based on a standard canon, an adult male measures between seven and eight heads in height, two in width, three for his arms, four for the legs, two to the knee, with the pubis at the middle of the total height.

The Modulor *of Le Corbusier, one of the first attempts at standardization of construction.*

Standard canon of proportions of the human body.

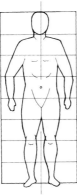

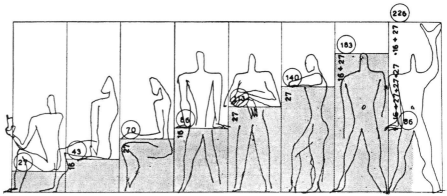

It is good practice to copy figures from magazines. Select examples with different points of view, shorter or taller, and observe the variation in their size and appearance.

Once this static skeleton is established, we articulate it and give the posture coherence in order to fill out the different parts of the body, approximating them to spherical or cylindrical surfaces which we then cover with clothing. However, the representations of people or groups must be more symbolic than realistic since, generally, the scale for architectural drawing does not permit many details. Except in studies of urban settings, stylized or indistinct figures in a well-defined pose are most commonly used so that they do not hinder the understanding of the architectural form. In sketches and studies in perspective, if the ground is horizontal, the eyes of all the people in the scene coincide with the eye of the observer at the horizon, diminishing in height as the distance increases. A good exercise is to copy from publications figures in different sizes and postures.

Examples of figures in different positions and representations by Carlos Conesa.

Thumbnail sketch by Carlos Conesa from the plans for the California Aerospace Museum, Los Angeles, California, by Frank Gehry. The human figure is always a reference of scale in architecture.

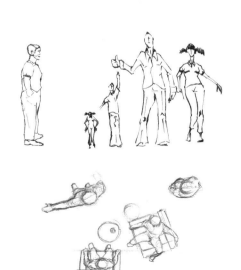

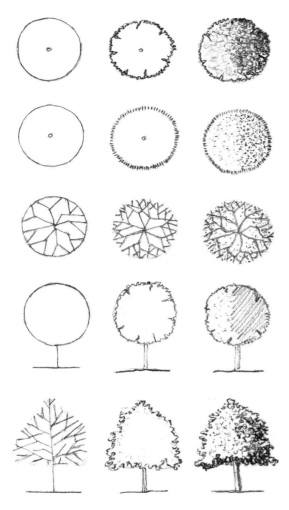

VEGETATION

Depending on the representation, its level of abstraction and the type of projection, we identify first the structure of the plant or its trunk and branches, then its volume or demeanor, and finally its mass and the texture of its foliage. Given the great variety of trees and shrubs that exists, the first task is to learn to draw some basic types—radial or amorphous structure, circular, pyramidal, or columnar—with a slender or stocky appearance, with uniform or disperse foliage, and with or without an appreciable texture to the leaves.

Secondly, given that organic forms grow logically from the ground upward, the drawing should reflect the characteristics of the lower branches, whose thickness increases closer to the trunk.

Finally, when a sample is not found in isolation but rather in a group or enclosure or among shrubs, its appearance in the scene must follow the same criteria, especially in the case of background, where the representation is even more simplified.

Normally, in the dimensioned sketch and the idea sketch, we use the most simplified representations, introducing the texture of the leaves in a very restrained manner. In a thumbnail sketch, a variety of expressions are used simultaneously, since the sensation of distance can be reinforced with one-point perspective, by means of forms that are rendered with more or less detail depending on the distance at which they are viewed.

To begin, we recommend drawing the most common examples of vegetation in the neighborhood, focusing on isolated trees as models. First study the leaves, whose shape will suggest the texture, and then draw the branches and the whole tree by itself. Later, try drawing groups of trees at increasing distances.

A selection of pencil sketches showing vegetation viewed at eye level and from above.

Other examples of plant elements.

Black-pencil thumbnail sketch of a rural landscape in Sant Martí Vell, Spain. The mass of the vegetation is achieved with shading.

The concepts explained here apply in establishing a scale of representation for vegetation, making use of geometric figures such as circles and triangles. No strict rules exist for this process, so it falls to the individual to devise a graphic range.

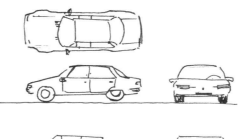

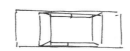

Ink thumbnail sketches of an olive tree progressing from the leaf to the whole and a group.

FURNISHINGS AND VEHICLES

Furnishings are described symbolically to communicate the use and size of different spaces. It is important to establish the surroundings or placement, the degree of detail depending on the scale of the drawing; too much detail and inappropriate placement interfere with the lines that define the architectural form. The use of vehicles is the same and the strategy identical, from the general outline to the detail: avoid excessive realism that distracts from or hides the quality of the building or space represented.

Vehicles and elements of urban furniture, such as streetlights, shown in a variety of styles.

dimensioning, Lettering
and composition of the drawing

as previously discussed, an architectural drawing is a scale representation of a reality or of the formal characteristics of a project, a graphic expression that has many versions. When the drawing constitutes an intermediate graphic expression, like a dimensioned sketch or an idea sketch, the base from which other drawings or ideas are developed, the architect must indicate more precisely the relationship between the representation and the corresponding reality or project. Drawing by its abstract nature is limited in describing the measurements and materials of its subjects. Therefore, we use dimensions, annotations, lettering, and symbols. In the case of a thumbnail drawing, the higher degree of realism allows the architect to limit the graphic register to titles and brief annotations.

Pencil dimensioned sketch from a fragment of the plan for a single-family home in Maia, Portugal, by Eduardo Souto de Moura. The sketch includes the horizontal dimensions and a variety of symbols.

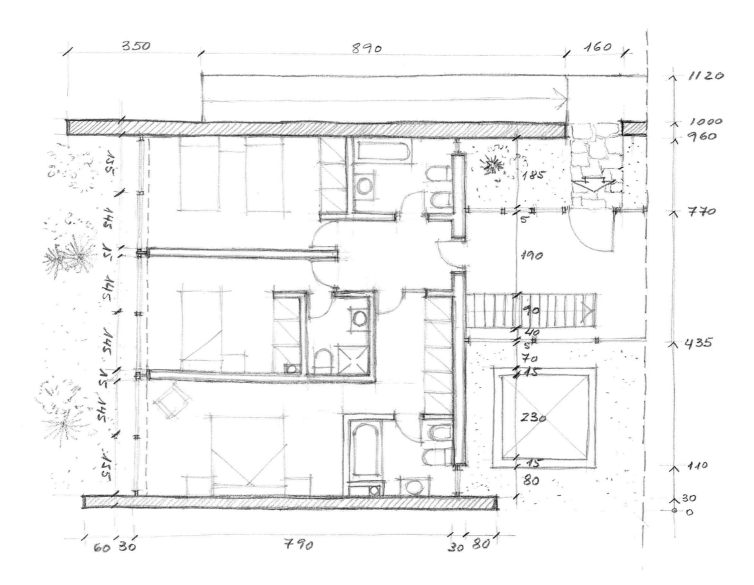

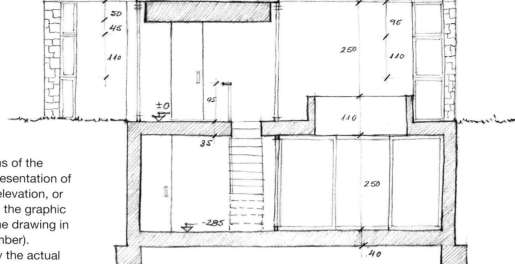

Pencil dimensioned sketch of a section from the plans for a single-family home, Maia, Portugal, by Eduardo Souto de Moura. The sketch includes the vertical dimensions.

DIMENSIONS

Measurements give the actual dimensions of the subject, and they enhance the scale representation of an orthogonal projection, whether plan, elevation, or section. Consequently, their location and the graphic expression must be complementary to the drawing in every sense (placement, weight, and number). The measurements represent numerically the actual dimensions of the subjects and they are placed along a subordinate dimension line that is parallel, equal, and referenced to the axes of the structure to be surveyed. The ends are marked with a distinguishing line or symbol in order to make them evident. In curved forms of constant radius, the measurement defines the radius and the angle described, and is marked next to the curve. The measurement can define the total length of one part of the form, called a general dimension, or it can be a part of the whole, known as a partial dimension. A third set of measurements is cumulative, where an entire series of dimensions is expressed as partial distances from a common point of origin. Whatever method is used, the fundamental issue is that the drawing be accurate, without producing any uncertainty, so that another person can reproduce the information. When the drawing deals with the general order or particular modular parts of a building, the dimensions can be provided more generically.

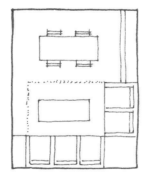
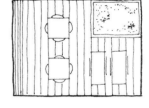
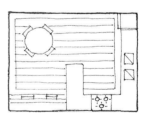

Some symbols representing the common architectural elements and complementary ones.

GRAPHIC SYMBOLS

In the dimensioned sketch, some elements of information are represented on a proportionally different scale—for example, when their size is very small. Examples are symbols that represent particular technical equipment, entrances, the direction of ascent of a staircase or ramp, the direction of north, or, in the form of a graphic scale, the real dimensions of the subject. This information is communicated with symbols whose location and size should fit with the drawing as a whole.

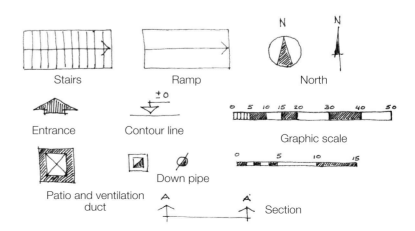

Stairs · Ramp · North · Entrance · Contour line · Graphic scale · Patio and ventilation duct · Down pipe · Section

Catalog of roman letters designed at the Bauhaus.

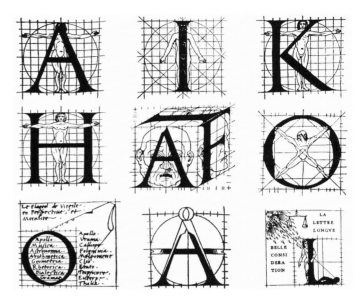

Catalog of roman letters, by G. Tory (fifteenth century).

Two examples of historical interest: the design of letters from the Renaissance to the Bauhaus.

LETTERING

Annotations verbally describe material qualities, instructions for building, the type of projection, or other data of interest. Titles provide the name of the drawing, its designer, the project, the projection. Titles are located adjacent to the drawing so that the whole forms a coherent composition and does not cause confusion. The lettering sets the label style and is drawn, not written. Therefore, its dimensions are laid out and proportioned in a particular scope and place, and its value is determined by applying greater or lesser thickness to the lines or strokes depending on their importance.

The process of lettering involves the basic sketching of horizontal guide lines, including lines to indicate the midpoint, which determines the height of the capital or lowercase letters. The letters can be tall, normal, or short, depending on whether the intermediate axis is above, centered at, or below the middle of the total height of the letter.

Vertical guide lines allow for the proper distribution of the letters, which must be adjusted to the space reserved for labels while the negative spaces are balanced. This is known as uniform spacing. The spacing should also take into account that not all the letters are inscribed in the same size block (the narrowest, i, l, 1 . . . and punctuation marks occupy the least space). This is known as proportional spacing.

The proportions and orientation of the height and width of a letter, along with the location of the midpoint, determine its style. As we propose freehand and rapid drawing, we will not focus on these distinctions, but we do insist that everyone label with lettering that is comfortable and easy to read at a normal distance. Its size should emphasize the importance of the label without detracting from the illustration.

A series of parallel guide lines works best for labeling. The lines should not be very long, since they are difficult to manage when drawn freehand.

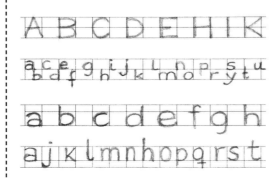

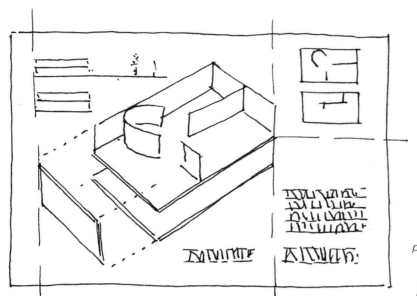

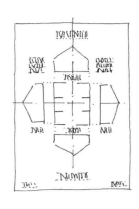

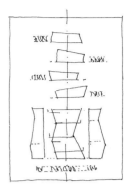

Different arrangements and possibilities for composition of a sketch and complementary lettering, ensuring visual balance, harmony, and legibility of the whole.

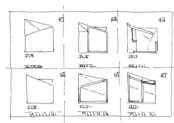

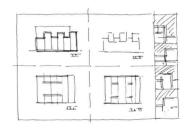

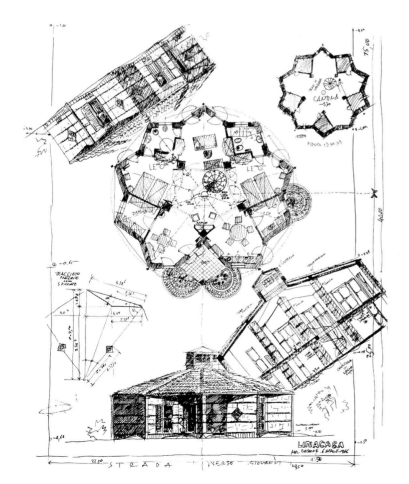

COMPOSITION

The drawing as a whole should form an organized visual image on the paper so that the labels and symbols occupy free spaces near the area to which they refer. In the case of the dimensioned sketch, this arrangement applies to the drawing, measurements, labeling, and symbols; in other cases, to the titles or annotations. Titles can be placed in a conventional way, at the foot of the sheet, or according to some compositional criterion, reinforcing the symmetry, order, or arrangement of the drawing.

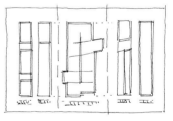

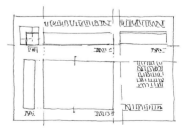

Ink dimensioned sketch by Mario Ridolfi. A good example of the composition of different architectural representations on a sheet.

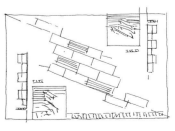

the dimensioned
Sketch
Capturing geometry
and measuring reality

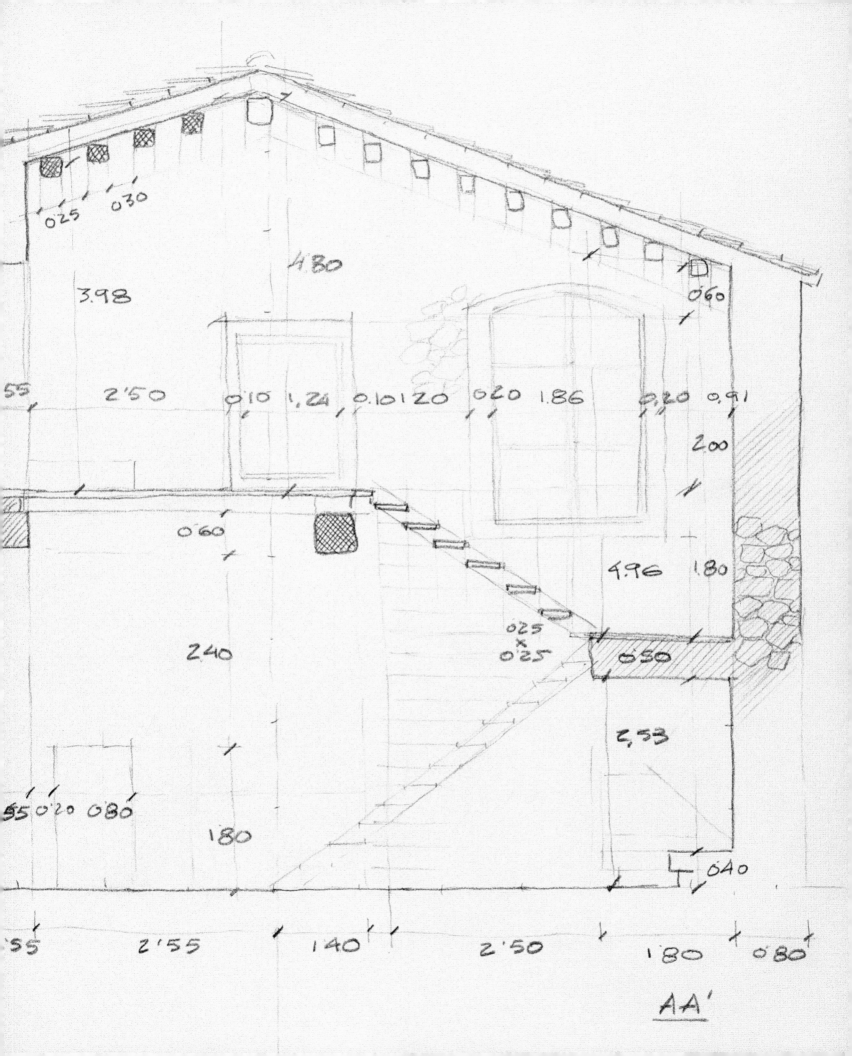

0'25   0'30

4.80

3.98

'55   2'50   0.10 1,24   0.10 1.20   0.20   1.86   0.20 0.91

0.60

2.00

4.96   1.80

0'60

2'40   0'25
            x
            0'25   0'50

2.53

'55 0'20 0'80

1'80   0'40

'55   2'55   1'40   2'50   1'80   0'80

AA'

Basic principles
of the dimensioned

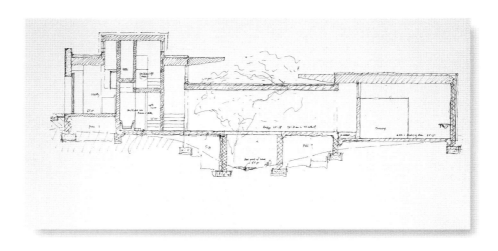

WILLIAMS TSIEN
SECTION OF A HOUSE IN THE DESERT, PHOENIX, ARIZONA.
DIMENSIONED SKETCH.

sketch

The dimensioned sketch is a freehand drawing

executed with a certain speed and with an instrument that responds easily to the pressure of the hand and the modulations of its movement. The objective of the dimensioned sketch is to represent one or more essential characteristics of the architectural project that we are trying to analyze and describe in order to present information about its dimensions and materials as a basis for drawing plans to scale. We are talking about a field drawing, with its own character as a technical drawing, so that linear values, lines, measurements, and annotations describe a project or an architectural reality, using common methods of projection, plans, elevations, sections, etc., executed entirely freehand, with less graphic precision but no less rigor.

The dimensioned sketch must therefore be rigorous in the methods of projection and in the correspondence of the projections; and the dimensions must define the geometry of the model accurately.

Systems
of representation

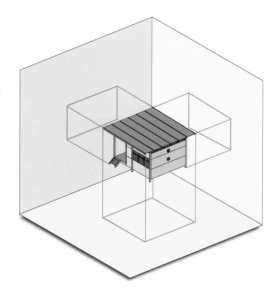

Diagram of how the points in the orthographic projection system are projected orthogonally (at 90º).

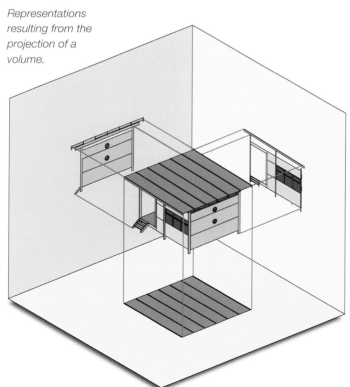

Representations resulting from the projection of a volume.

any architectural element can be drawn in two dimensions by means of graphic conventions called systems of representation. Among them the orthographic, the axonometric, and the linear perspective stand out. The orthographic system is differentiated from the other two in that it is based on the representation of forms by means of diverse projections or simultaneous points of view, which is to say, not in a natural manner, and it is necessary to interpret them all in order to get an idea of the total volume. The other two systems, on the other hand, are based on the representation of the element from a single point of view, similar to its volumetric appearance. The difference between the second two systems lies in that, in the axonometric system, the edges that are parallel in reality remain parallel in the projection, whereas in the linear perspective system parallel lines converge, generally at the vanishing points, unless they are frontal, in which case they remain parallel.

REPRESENTATION THROUGH MULTIPLE VIEWS

The orthographic system used in technical drawing is based on the concept that the projections or views of the object stem from points of view in the infinite, and they are projected on planes perpendicular to each other.
Thus arise the top, right, left, bottom, and rear views depending on the projected direction, predominantly views from the outside, except when a slice or section of the object is projected. These perpendicular views are called elevations, which will be principal or lateral, or, depending on their orientation, north, south, east, or west. The top view is called the roof plan, and all together these views describe the external appearance of the building.

Roof

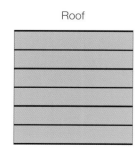

The roof of the building after its vertical projection.

 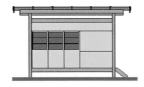 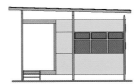 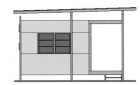

These are the four elevations that are obtained by projecting the volume horizontally.

The concepts covered on these pages warrant close attention, especially the representations resulting from the different "visions" of a single architectural element, because they constitute the basis for the orthographic description.

Architecture creates spaces, and for that purpose the vertical and horizontal cuts are fundamental. The vertical cuts display the height of the different spaces as well as the visual relationship between the different levels. And the horizontal cuts describe the uses of the different spaces, access to them, and circulation through them.

The vertical cuts are called sections, and their name varies according to their location within the total volume. They may be transverse or longitudinal sections. Sections are also created from selected cuts along planes that pass through elements of volume that might be of interest for the description of the volume. We indicate this plane by means of a mark drawn on the plan.

When the form is very symmetrical, the section ideally follows the axes of symmetry.

We call horizontal cuts plans; their height indicates the different plans that together compose the volume.

On plans, the plane of cut lies at approximately 1.5 m (5 ft) from the floor of each level, so that the doors, windows, furniture, etc. can be distinguished from the walls.

In order to see the interior we need to cut the volume along particular planes.

Representations resulting from projecting a volume cut along the planes that cross it.

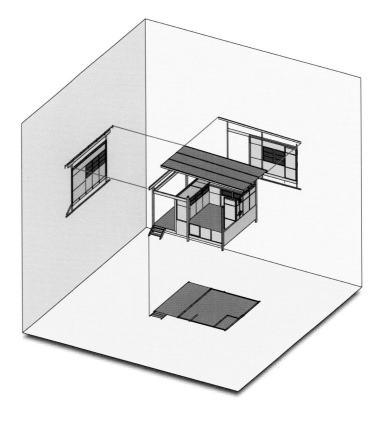

Plan

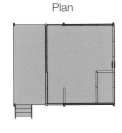

The plan of the volume is the vertical projection of the cut along a horizontal plane.

*Arrangement of
views flattening the
planes into the
shape of a flower.*

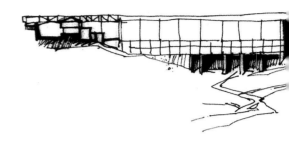

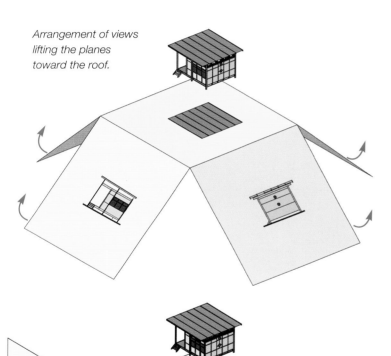

*Arrangement of views
lifting the planes
toward the roof.*

GRAPHIC CONVENTIONS

The existence of graphic conventions stems from the need to standardize the graphic language of architecture so that it may be understood by all.

For example, all the edges that define the planes or boundaries and that are seen directly should be drawn with continuous lines. Discontinuous lines should be used to draw anything hidden or concealed by the plane of cut, as long as it cannot be seen in any of the other representations; otherwise, the profusion of lines will impede an accurate understanding.

ARRANGEMENT OF VIEWS

The arrangement of views is governed by very simple criteria. The first, for its ease of layout, results from the disassembly of the different projections on a single horizontal plane—that of the floor—similar to flattening the petals of a flower around its center. But this results in an inverted image of the object, obliging the observer to change position or turn the paper in order to understand the design. A second procedure resolves this problem by raising the projections toward the plane of the roof, thus avoiding an inverted view and diminishing the problem of seeing one of the elevations face down. An alternative is to position the projections one after another, like an accordion. When the architectural structure is very complex and, especially, for non-orthogonal forms (forms not perpendicular to each other), auxiliary views or projections with respect to other planes can be generated, but they must be clearly defined.

*Projections arranged
consecutively.*

REPRESENTING THE SITE

Another of the peculiarities of architectural drawing is that the line of the earth or ground level, the horizontal axis of coordinates of the spatial model, becomes the site anchoring the construction. This is never totally horizontal, so a simplified version of the orthographic projection system is used, called the elevation. It uses contour lines or flat horizontal sections of the terrain at different heights to represent the terrain and is complemented by different vertical sections that show the relationship between the height of the building and its surroundings.

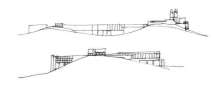

Dimensioned sketch by Emili Donato showing sections of the CIAC, Santiago de Compostela, Spain, on a very uneven site.

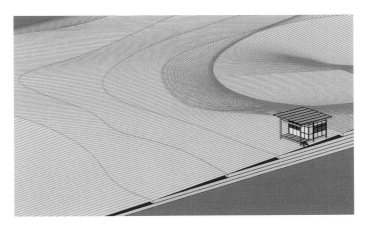

Contour lines and vertical sections in the representation of a site.

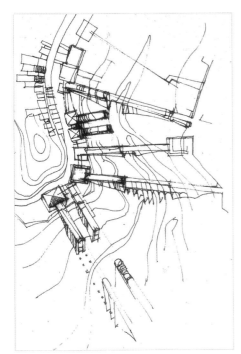

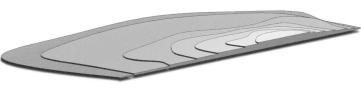

Dimensioned sketch by Emili Donato that reflects the curves of level of the CIAC, Santiago de Compostela, Spain.

the axonometric system affords a unique view of architectural volume from an outside point, using its projection along a single direction in such a way that the projecting lines are parallel to each other. If the direction is perpendicular to the drawing plane, the result is an orthogonal axonometric projection. If, on the other hand, the direction is oblique with respect to the plane, the result is an oblique axonometric projection. The difference with respect to the orthographic projection system is that the observer perceives the object along a single direction that does not coincide with the object's planes of reference; nor are as many views required in order to describe the object. The result is a view in which the straight lines remain parallel, distorting the angles. It can be measured only on the axes of reference, which in general do not preserve the orthogonal quality in the projection.

Fundamentals of axonometry

ORTHOGONAL AXONOMETRIC PERSPECTIVES

The most common perspectives in this group are isometrics, in which the three axes of reference form equal angles. Also common are dimetrics, in which two of the angles form axes that are equal with respect to the paper or the drawing, and trimetrics, in which the three angles are different. For convenience we will only work with the isometric perspective, without applying reduction. Drawing them stems from the definition of a triad of axes with one direction. The most common triad is of 120° between axes, an intuitive way. The inconvenient aspect of this triad is that too much superimposition and even some visual confusion occur with very symmetrical architecture.

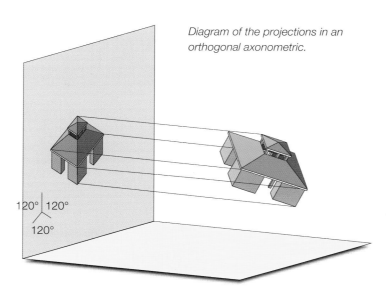

Diagram of the projections in an orthogonal axonometric.

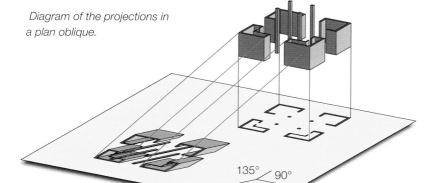

Diagram of the projections in a plan oblique.

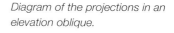
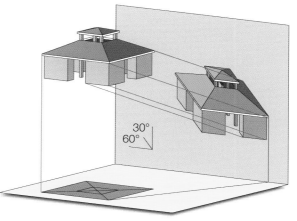

Diagram of the projections in an elevation oblique.

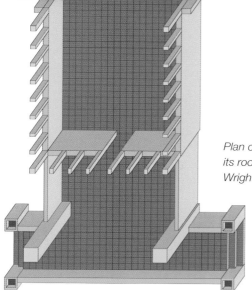

Plan oblique of the terrace without its roof, house by Frank Lloyd Wright.

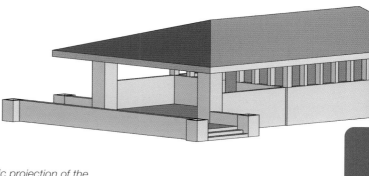

Orhogonal axonometric projection of the terrace of a house by Frank Lloyd Wright.

OBLIQUE
AXONOMETRIC PERSPECTIVES

Of this group we will only consider those in which one of the object's planes of reference is parallel to the observer's plane of reference, and its projection on the plane is angled, although the rays of projection are still parallel to each other. In this group are the elevation oblique, when the elevation or section is parallel to the paper, and the plan oblique, when the plan is parallel to the paper. One starts from the elevation, the plan, or the section, and the other edges extend or elevate, forming an angle, ideally between 30° and 60°. The range of possibilities is very broad, but selection is limited to those triads that produce believable views with little distortion, a further consideration when working freehand and in an intuitive way. Without doubt, what counts is practice and perceptual experience.

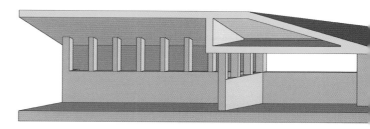

Section oblique of the terrace of a house by Frank Lloyd Wright.

Isometric of a single-family house in Germany by David Chipperfield.

Plan oblique of the Steir House, Garches, France, by Le Corbusier.

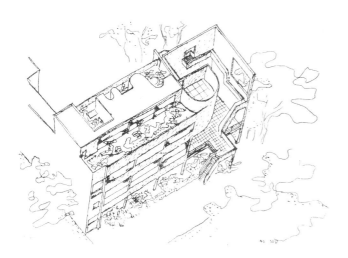

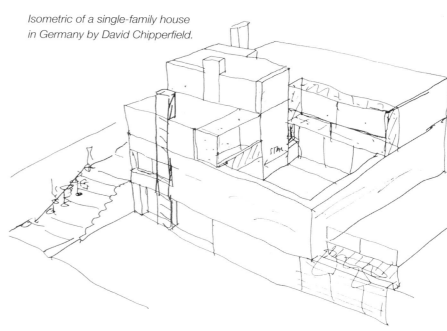

the dimensioned Sketch
in axonometric perspective

axonometric perspective is a more intuitive and simple representation than orthographic projections because any architectural form can be described with a single image. Because it maintains the parallelism and proportions among the different parts of the object, not its angles, the axonometric has become common practice. In a dimensioned sketch, for example, we can describe and take measurements of an element from an elevated point of view, capturing all of its proportions. Generally, this is desirable to describe elements of furniture or decoration, as well as construction details, where the interrelationship of the parts is very important and takes precedence over the view of the whole.

RECOMMENDED VARIATIONS

The axonometrics most often used for freehand dimensioned sketches are the isometric, the plan oblique, and the elevation or section oblique. The isometric, with its angular configuration, closely resembles an intuitive view of the model, although in this case one cannot measure angles, and circular forms are represented as ellipses. When this occurs, and above all when information is available on the plan of the model, the best choice is the plan oblique, drawing the heights at an angle of between 30° and 60° with the plan. In both cases measurements can be taken, but only in the plan oblique or in its variant, the elevation oblique, do the dimensions and angles remain in the plane of reference. And they will be truly useful as long as the dimensions are arranged parallel to the axes of reference.

Pencil dimensioned sketch in orthogonal axonometric perspective of the Rietveld chair.

Chair designed by G. Rietveld.

Pencil dimensioned sketch in orthogonal axonometric showing horizontal sections of wood doors, one with glass and the other solid wood.

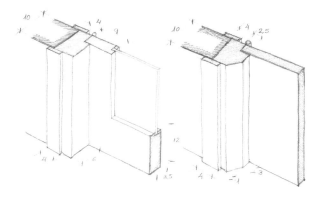

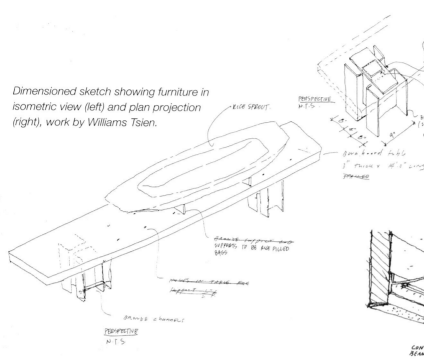

Dimensioned sketch showing furniture in isometric view (left) and plan projection (right), work by Williams Tsien.

Despite the fact that the common approach to a dimensioned sketch of furniture is to resort to the axonometric view, one can also use a section perspective if it is accompanied by dimensions and annotations.

When describing an unbuilt project, we recommend you make a dimensioned sketch of the whole building to describe the relationship between its different elements, showing them in an aerial view. The most common approach for a first volumetric study involves including only a few general dimensions or those that define a structural or decorative order.

The isometric is the most common projection because, as previously noted, it appears less distorted and more intuitive than oblique projections. Other representations of the plan and elevations generally accompany an isometric projection.

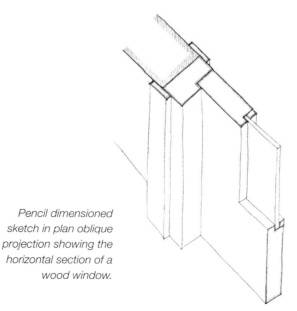

Pencil dimensioned sketch in elevation oblique showing the vertical section of a wood door with glass.

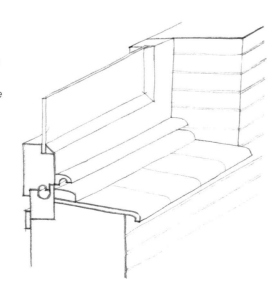

Pencil dimensioned sketch in plan oblique projection showing the horizontal section of a wood window.

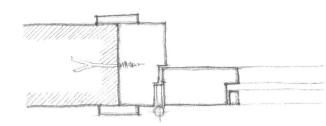

scale and Level of detail

every architectural element has certain dimensions whose representation requires the use of a graphic convention. Plans are therefore drawn in a similar and proportional way, based on a system of measurements of reference. In this system, a real unit of the building, one meter or one foot, is represented in the drawing as half that value (1/2), one fifth (1/5), one one-hundredth (1/100), and so on. When a drawing is made to 1/100 scale, each unit of the drawing is equivalent to 100 of the actual units. This is the concept behind the measurement scale employed in technical drawing.

RELATIVE SCALE

When drawing an architectural dimensioned sketch, the first consideration is the relative scale of the space that one wishes to represent and the size of the paper, defined as the visual, graphic, or perceptual scale. The larger the element to be drawn, the greater the reduction necessary for the projection to fit on the paper, and the lower the level of detail. Otherwise, as the need for detail increases, so does the size of the drawing; in other words, the visual or graphic scale, as well as the measurement scale, will be bigger.

Pencil dimensioned sketch showing the horizontal section of a wood window. In order to preserve the level of detail when the elements are too long, a valid strategy is to remove the intermediate areas by indicating a break along dotted lines.

Pencil sketch of a plan showing walls, doors, and windows with greater or lesser degree of simplification depending on the scale to which they are drawn.

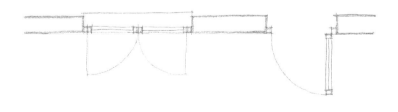

Pencil sketch showing the horizontal section of a plywood door.

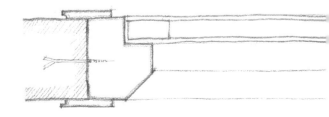

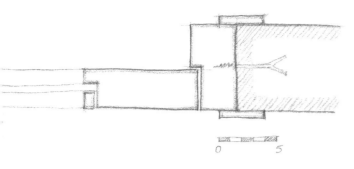

Pencil dimensioned sketch showing the horizontal section of a wood door with glass.

Pencil dimensioned sketch showing the vertical section of a wood window (A). Pencil dimensioned sketch showing the vertical section of a wood door with glass (B).

A   B

In the dimensioned sketch, the concept of scale is a little different. The dimensioned sketch is drawn without the help of a ruler, but rather with a guide or graphic scale that is laid over the paper and made equivalent to some element of the building, be it paving stones, columns, or other repetitive features.
In considering the level of detail, we talk about different scales: the actual scale (1/1), scales of detail, partial scales showing specific elements, and scales showing the whole. All of these complement one another, with a varying number of measurements depending on the degree of precision that one wants to provide. Another possibility is to include a graphic element of reference as a value for establishing an approximate measurement. For example, a human figure or some piece of furniture, like a bed or a table, whose dimensions with respect to the human being are easily recognized. This strategy is known as drawing to human scale. The height of a person or of the observer with respect to its surroundings, human steps, feet, or handbreadths are used to measure the setting that is represented, incorporating a simplified human figure in the sketch in order to describe the relative scale of the drawing.

Pencil sketch of an elevation and vertical section of a wood door with glass and its relation to human scale.

Pencil dimensioned sketch of the Fueter House in Switzerland by Le Corbusier, showing a plan and its relationship to human scale.

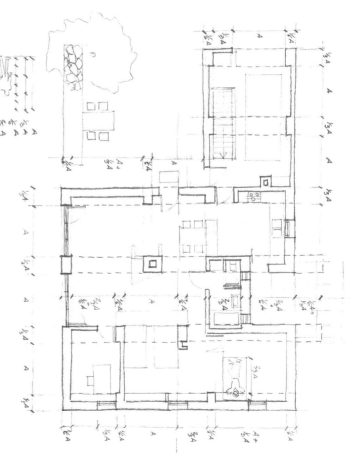

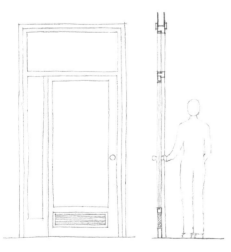

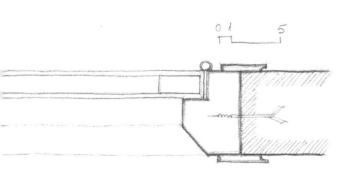

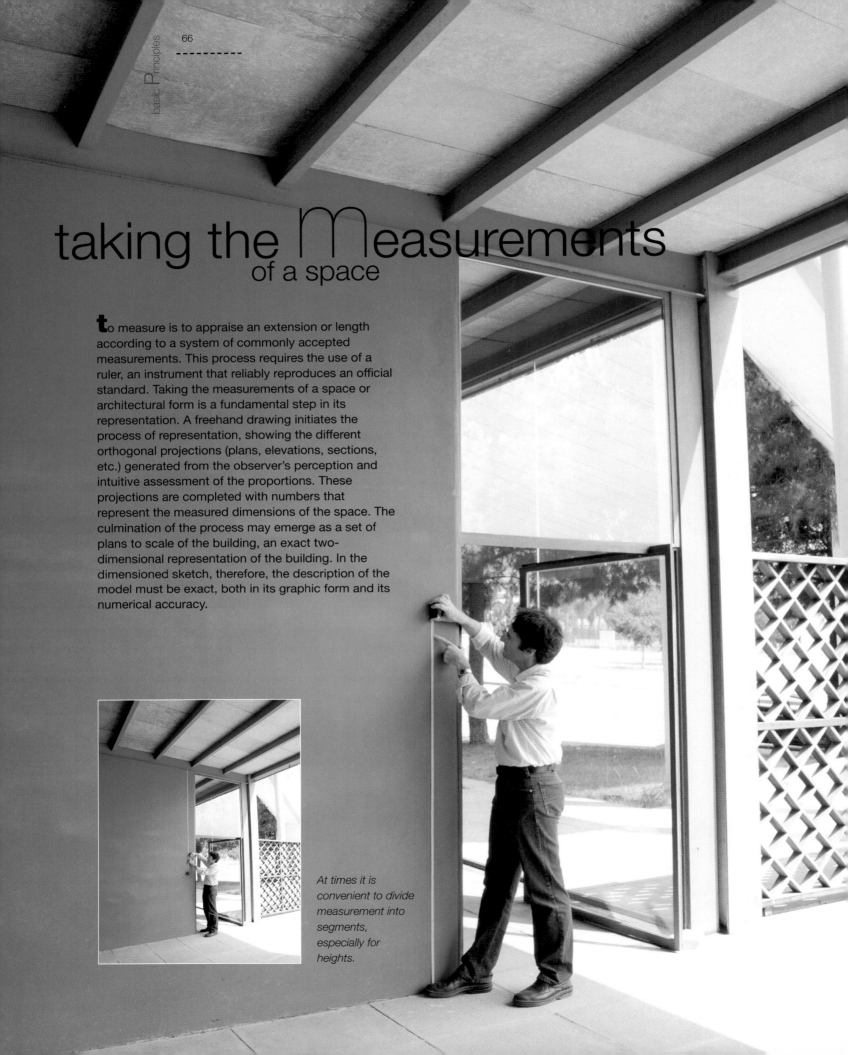

taking the Measurements
of a space

to measure is to appraise an extension or length according to a system of commonly accepted measurements. This process requires the use of a ruler, an instrument that reliably reproduces an official standard. Taking the measurements of a space or architectural form is a fundamental step in its representation. A freehand drawing initiates the process of representation, showing the different orthogonal projections (plans, elevations, sections, etc.) generated from the observer's perception and intuitive assessment of the proportions. These projections are completed with numbers that represent the measured dimensions of the space. The culmination of the process may emerge as a set of plans to scale of the building, an exact two-dimensional representation of the building. In the dimensioned sketch, therefore, the description of the model must be exact, both in its graphic form and its numerical accuracy.

At times it is convenient to divide measurement into segments, especially for heights.

More rigid tapes are used or, in some cases, a small electronic measurer, in order to take vertical measurements.

MEASUREMENTS

To begin with, there is an important distinction between measurements of direction and distance. Measurements indicate the distances between the different parts of the building, taken by following along the walls or between them. However, these values are not precise unless they are accompanied by the directions or the angles formed between them.

Different strategies and instruments can be used in taking measurements. The choice depends upon the extent to be measured.

The first measurements are the general horizontal ones of the plan (taken with long, flexible measuring tapes), then come the partial measurements (taken with smaller, rigid measuring tapes), which must always refer to a known point of origin. The flexible tapes only allow for the measurement of low heights because they tend to collapse easily when extended. Another solution is to divide measurement into segments, starting with a point of reference.

We can begin by measuring with paces, counting paving stones, boundaries, or other features, since all of these will help to frame and proportion the final drawing, but they will not be very precise values.

When measuring heights greater than 3 m (10 ft), we use an extendable tape from the ground, or an electronic measurer, a surveying instrument. When the roof is accessible, a tape can be dropped from above, although this method is inconvenient because the intermediate dimensions are not easily found.

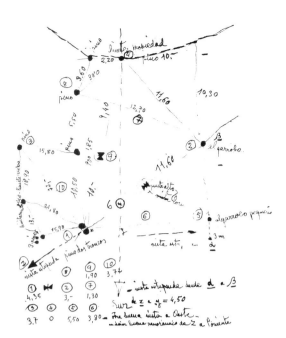

*Dimensioned sketch by Josep Antoni
Coderch of the surroundings and woodland
of the Ugalde House I, Barcelona, Spain.*

*Sometimes even a sketchbook can help take
perpendicular measurements of a given
element.*

SURVEYING

When dealing with limited spaces, the angles are not measured with
sophisticated apparatus like tachymeters or other instruments designed for
surveying; however, these spaces are too large to measure with
instruments for technical drawing like protractors. Instead, we use the
strategy of triangulation, calculating the dimensions of the extension of a wall with the
measurement that results from the distance between its two ends and a third common point of
reference. This process, when applied to each of the walls, provides an exact representation of
the model.

One strategy to determine with a measuring tape whether two walls form a right angle consists of
defining a triangle whose sides measure 3, 4, and 5 meters or feet. The end of the tape is placed on
the ground at the corner formed by the walls. Then 3 meters or feet are measured along one of the
walls from that point and marked with a piece of colored tape; then 4 meters or feet are measured
from the corner along the other wall and this second point is marked. If the angle is a right angle,
then the distance between the two marks should be 5 meters or feet. If the length is greater, the
angle will be greater than 90º, and if it is less, the angle will be less than 90º. The process for
calculating angles of inclination is similar and involves simply measuring the two legs of the triangle
that define distance and height with respect to the point of origin. If the wall is curved, and
therefore contains many directions, the solution involves a combination of strategies. First, an
orthogonal reference grid or spaced triangulations at equal intervals must be defined. Then different
points of the wall are measured along a single horizontal line. Finding the radius of a circular
element, like a column, is easier; simply divide its perimeter dimension by 2π .

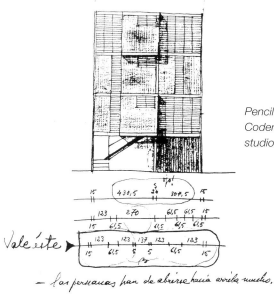

Pencil dimensioned sketch by Josep Antoni Coderch of the facade of Antoni Tàpies's studio, Barcelona, Spain.

The distance between two end points and a third point of common reference gives a single solution since a triangle is the only polygon that can be constructed from its sides, without the need for angles.

The process for finding an angle of inclination is simply to measure the height from the ground of the two ends of the inclined plane and the length of the wall.

We define an orthogonal reference grid and measure the different points of a curved wall in relation to the same horizontal line.

the dimensioned Sketch
step by step

the first step is to examine the place, noticing if the shape is orthogonal or presents some twist, if there are repetitive elements like pavements, columns, and so forth that might act as a guide and a first indication of the human scale of the space. If these clues are not present, it can be measured by pacing. Then the paper is divided into areas equivalent to the number of projections: plan, elevation, section, etc. of the subject, positioned relative to the plan that will occupy the central place.

When you have an idea of the size and how the projections should be oriented, the width of the sheet is divided into as many units as contained in the width of the plan, adding three additional units for each elevation, assuming a height of 2.7 m (9 ft) and a pace of 90 cm (35 in) and leaving a couple more units at each side for labels. The grid generated by the units (paces or paving stones) serves as a base, drawn very lightly on the page. The plan is drawn first, and then the different elevations. A clear hierarchy is established by varying the intensity of the line for the different elements—layout lines, axes of symmetry, partitions, walls, etc. Also represented with dotted lines are the hidden edges and the projections of the roof.

If the space is very symmetrical, the sketch can be simplified by dividing the plan into halves so that one shows the floor, for example, and the other, the roof. Or, one half displays the outlines and the other, the details of the floor.

Views of the entrance to the ground floor of the Pabellón de la República, Barcelona, Spain, by Josep Lluis Sert.

Detail of the main door.

1. The lines that define the different elements are laid out and drawn lightly over the grid.

1

2

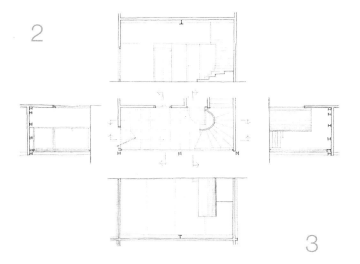

2. The ensemble is defined and weights of lines are chosen.

3. Next the sketch is completed by clearly defining any construction details that might be of interest.

Preparatory layout of the paper according to the dimensions of the subject—that is, the grid where the different drawings are placed—should be done with very light-weight lines that do not interfere with the rest of the drawing.

3

Finally, the different dimensions are taken, first the overall ones and then the partial ones, and they are indicated along the margins of the plans, oriented so that there is no need to turn the paper in order to read them. The resulting drawing will be to a graphic scale—that is, proportioned according to the units of the grid. The proportion and layout must be done correctly, since when the dimensions are noted, any disproportions will become evident.

The dimension lines and their labels should complement the principal drawing and not overwhelm it by their size and weight.

Leftover space on the paper can be used for small sketches of details, as well as for written descriptions; these should be annotated or labeled so that the information is clear.

4

4. The result should be a precise but agile drawing that describes the different walls, elements of the space, and their details, properly measured and labeled.

as discussed in the introduction to this chapter, a dimensioned sketch is a drawing with an expression peculiar to technical drawing—that is, with line weights, shading, dimensions, and annotations all for the purpose of describing an architectural project. Common methods of projection are used, but they are executed freehand, more descriptive of content than graphically precise.

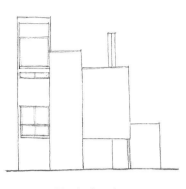

North elevation

the dimensioned Sketch
in architecture

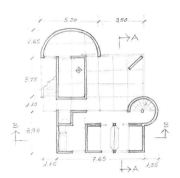

Ground floor

Traditionally, the dimensioned sketch has been used for surveying and noting data about existent buildings, or to communicate instructions that permit someone else to draw plans and execute them. In this sense, the dimensioned sketch is a drawing that closely approximates the manual process of construction, in its form of execution (generally on foot), its rigor and precision, and its methodology. The dimensioned sketch is definitively a drawing of instructions. First one thing is done, then another related to the first and, if necessary, measurements, labels, or some details supplement this. The progression is from the general to the particular, but without a margin of doubt and shaping a whole that does not permit many interruptions. It is, therefore, a drawing that is both narrative and calligraphic.

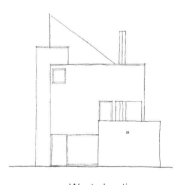

East elevation

Second floor

Pencil sketches showing the elevations in the plans for the Gwathmey House, Amagansett, New York, by Charles Gwathmey.

West elevation

Third floor

Pencil sketches showing the floor plans from the same project.

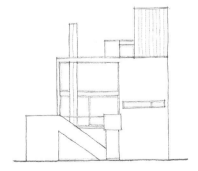

South elevation

USES OF THE DIMENSIONED SKETCH

The tradition of the dimensioned sketch of the plan, elevation, and section for the study of architecture, measuring and drawing, has been lost little by little as photography and specialized publications have become increasingly available to the general public. Nonetheless, its practice is still indispensable for anyone who is learning about architecture.

In the professional domain, the dimensioned sketch continues to play an essential part in the initial phases of a project, in the first steps of collecting intuitive measurements for the spaces, or in gathering data about existing buildings. Axonometric projection is usually used more for describing the whole, the volume of the work, the relationship of its elements, or the process of assembly and construction of the architectural work.

The dimensioned sketch is definitely very appropriate for situations in which the whole is given priority over the parts, in modular structures or those composed of complex volumes. In these cases the sketch is neither so rigid nor so complete. Isometric projection is generally used because it is a very intuitive approach that can be lightly dimensioned as a complement to other views, diagrams, and annotations.

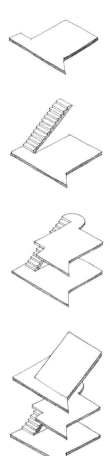
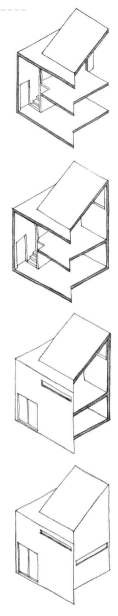

Ink sketches in orthogonal axonometric showing the process of joining architectural elements from the plans for Charles Gwathmey's studio, Amagansett, New York.

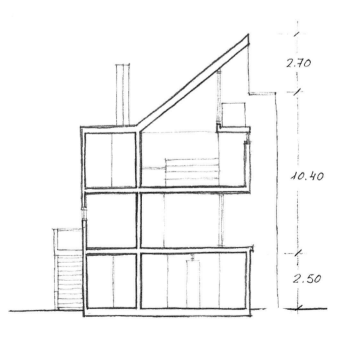
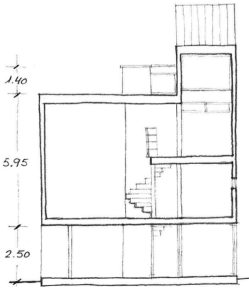

Pencil dimensioned sketches showing sections from the plans for the Gwathmey House.

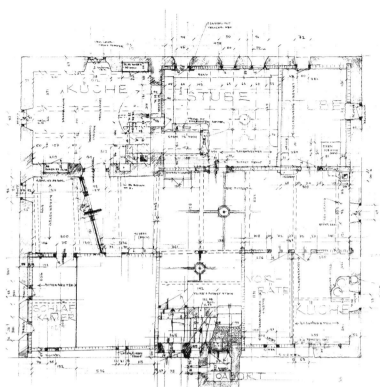

Dimensioned sketch of the plan of a typical house in Switzerland by Peter Zumthor.

DESIGNER'S DIMENSIONED SKETCH

As a personal drawing or one intended for a professional collaborator, the graphic quality of the dimensioned sketch is not given priority. However, some designers prefer the dimensioned sketch even for project presentation or for the description of certain kinds of architectures, like popular and historical structures, modern reinterpretations of them, or those that include fine craftsmanship.

One example is the classic sketch by Peter Zumthor that shows the plan of a typical Swiss mountain home with all its details. Another example is the sampling of projects drawn entirely freehand by a team of architects under the direction of Ludovico Quaroni. They show a variety of plans, elevations, and sections that exhibit the influence of the cultural movement of Italian realism in architecture.

Dimensioned sketches of the village of La Martella by Ludovico Quaroni, Matera, Italy.

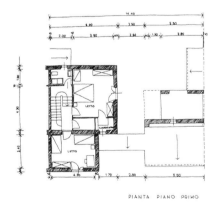

PIANTA PIANO PRIMO

PROSPETTO ANTERIORE

PROSPETTO POSTERIORE

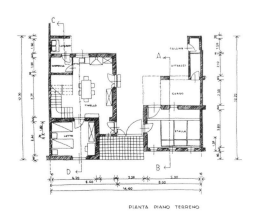

PIANTA PIANO TERRENO

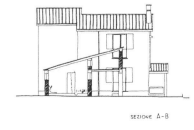

SEZIONE A-B

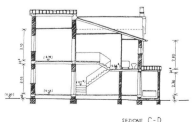

SEZIONE C-D

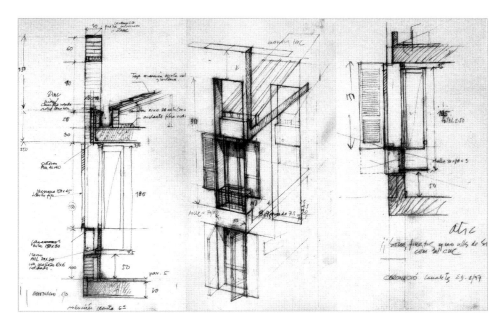

The perfection with which the architects executed these examples of the dimensioned sketch would lead one to think that they used precision instruments. However, this was not the case, testimony to the designers' mastery and level of graphic preparation.

Dimensioned sketch of details showing the facade and woodwork of housing in Canaletas by Emili Donato, Cerdanyola del Valles, Spain.

If in fact the dimensioned sketch is preferred in the early stages of an architectural project, it also constitutes a great tool for the analysis and transmission to others of architectural solutions for details pertaining to the last stages of the planning process. In it are gathered together almost all of the facets, from mere linear representation to a written report describing or explaining the intentions, to labeling, line weights, shading, and shadow. The important personal aspect of the drawing is apparent in the two examples on this page, both showing details. Here Arne Jacobsen and Emili Donato analyze partial elements of an architectural project, but the individual technique and the use of graphic resources produce different results, very distinct forms of narration. Nonetheless, with regard to the architectural content, both speak the same language.

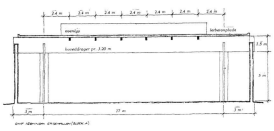

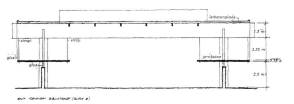

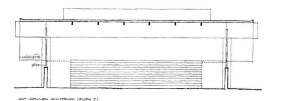

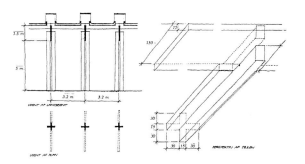

Dimensioned sketch showing sections and construction details of St. Catherine's and Merton College, Oxford, England, by Arne Jacobsen.

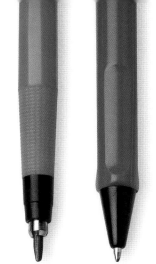

Using the dimensioned sketch.

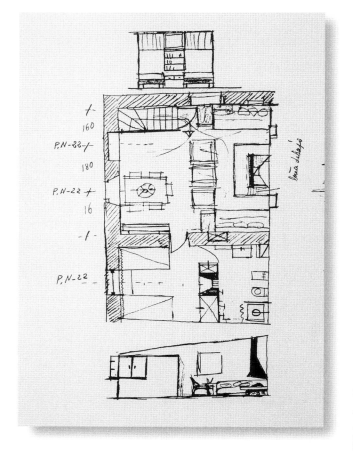

JOSEP ANTONI CODERCH.
RESTORATION OF A HOUSE IN CADAQUES, GIRONA, SPAIN.
DIMENSIONED SKETCH.

Common cases.

The conditions we might encounter

when preparing a dimensioned sketch are quite varied, depending as much on the content and style of the architectural model as on its particular complexity.

In the interest of offering some typical examples of the dimensioned sketch, we will start with the survey of an interior with complex forms.

The next example will be a study of an exterior setting or patio of a monumental building, incorporating vegetation and representing the surrounding facades.

The final example, the restoration of a historic building, shows a modern addition to a structure of traditional architecture.

an Interior space
in the dimensioned sketch

Exterior view of the expansion of the Escuela Técnica Superior de Arquitectura de Barcelona.

this particular space is a part of the expansion of the Escuela Técnica Superior de Arquitectura de Barcelona, the work of J. A. Coderich, from 1979. The designer, in the last years of his career, began to play with the juxtaposition of the prismatic forms of the original building and other more organic forms that would act as a transition to the surroundings. He gave shape to them as undulating vertical enclosures, covering their exterior with ceramic tiles and the interior with white plaster. These features were combined with black woodwork in an irregular prismatic pattern that, in the windows, lies over planters, with the idea that the vegetation would flow onto the different surfaces. The result is a series of fluid spaces of curvilinear design that generate some very suggestive spatial sequences and noticeable light play, since all the natural light and a good part of the artificial light bathe the surfaces at a low angle. The walls of these settings are closed to the outdoors in order to encourage the students' ability to concentrate.

Interior view showing the rest and study area in the expansion of the Escuela Técnica Superior de Arquitectura, Barcelona, Spain, by Josep Antoni Coderch.

Pencil sketch showing the footprint of the space to be studied in reference to its closest surroundings.

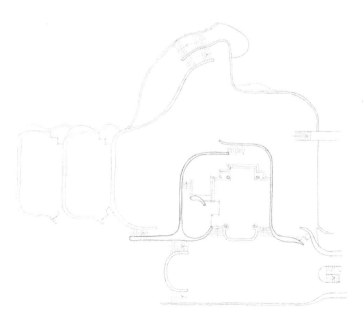

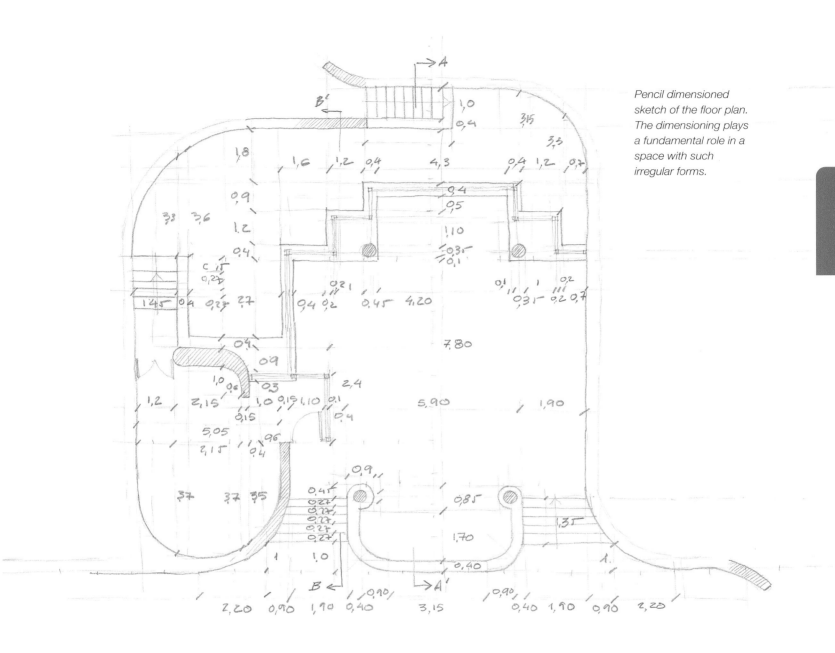

Pencil dimensioned sketch of the floor plan. The dimensioning plays a fundamental role in a space with such irregular forms.

FOCUS AND STEPS TO FOLLOW

In creating a series of dimensioned sketches of this interior, the work centers around a part of the vestibule, an area for rest and study, which provides a good indication of the other spaces of the project. The process requires, thus, an initial examination, pacing out the grid of the building that is then reflected in a small diagram or very schematic sketch. This will provide a frame of reference for the different areas of focus and an understanding of the general order and magnitude of the whole project.

The principal challenge in surveying or taking measurements and then drawing the sketch of spaces with such free forms is to set the axes of reference in a way that facilitates representation of the curves, since these are not constant. A further challenge is how to connect the different settings across a series of partial sketches; a detailed sketch of the whole building cannot fit onto a single 11- by 17-inch (297- by 420-mm) sheet.

Some general axes of reference for the whole building are defined along the halls in a rectilinear pattern, with other axes specific to each setting arranged as branches, coinciding clearly with the access doors for each area as well as the joints of the pavement, edges, slopes, etc., which are marked, if necessary, in chalk on the ground.

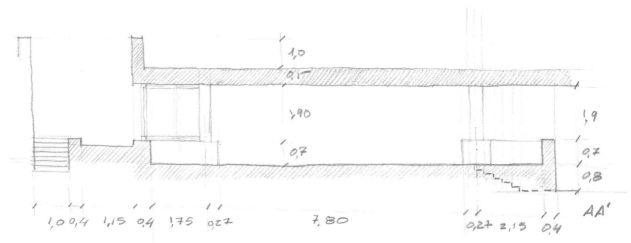

Pencil dimensioned sketch of the section A-A' from the preceding page describing the vertical space.

Once these axes have been considered in a general way with paces or by means of a tape measure extended on the floor, they are then transferred onto paper. In the first approximation, the distance is measured from the axes to the walls and then the drawing is laid out on the paper. Next, the space is adapted to a more or less regular shape, which is set on the paper with very light lines. Given the complexity of the subject, more than one sheet of paper is necessary for the plan and elevations.

At this point, one can tell at a glance, and from the axis of reference, when an exterior wall changes in curvature or orientation. The distances are measured with respect to the axis at every meter, foot, or pace, increasing the number of measurements depending on the complexity, so that for each segment of curve at least its ends and an intermediate point or step are known. This second stage of refinement, using a very fine lead without pressure, allows the curves to be drawn within the framework and, to some degree, lays the foundation of the dimensioned sketch.

Pencil dimensioned sketch of the section B-B', complementary to A-A'.

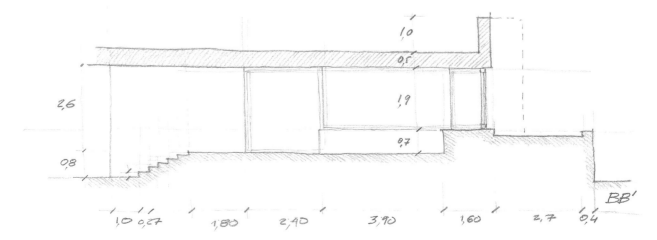

From here on, one must move through the structure and complete the remaining details of the sketch. This will also help to indicate characteristic features that can then be detailed in the margins of the drawing. Now is the time to assess and adjust the sectioned exterior walls, the changes of level, and the joints of the pavement with varying strokes and thicknesses, from greater to lesser. When this is finished, the axes of reference are marked, as dimensions have been measured to the exterior wall and, if necessary, intermediate values are defined. In the case of the curvilinear areas, if a measuring tape has been used as reference, measurements can be made to the origin, noting their value according to the measuring tape.

On a separate sheet of paper the sketch of a section marked on the plan is begun. The points along a cut are transferred to the edge of the sheet, along with any points that are above it. With this grid of dots copied onto the edge of the second sheet for reference, a section can be created once the height of the setting has been determined and considered.

Only a few of the most characteristic sketches done of this setting are shown, representing the plan, two sections, and two details—one of the articulated woodwork of the windows and the other showing the notation of a fragment of curved wall.

When there is too much information to fit in some detail of the sketch, it is best to create a sketch specific to that area. Otherwise the drawing would be illegible.

One of the curves of the space being studied. The pencil diagram shows how the elements are labeled.

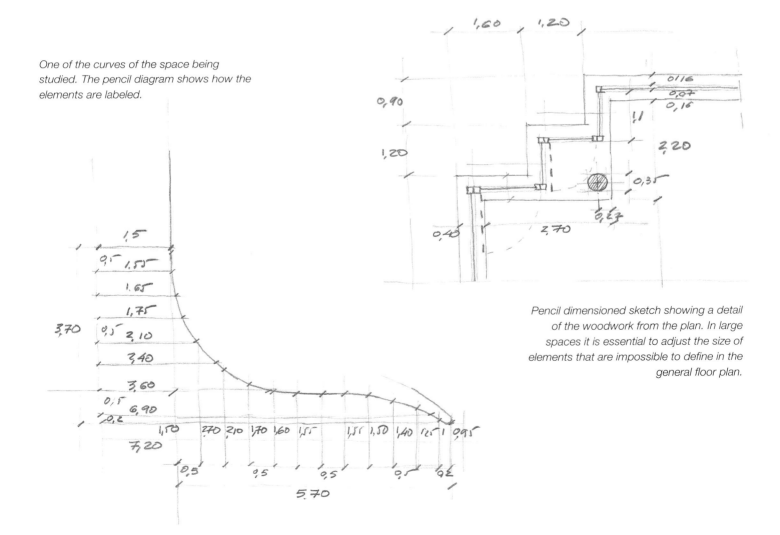

Pencil dimensioned sketch showing a detail of the woodwork from the plan. In large spaces it is essential to adjust the size of elements that are impossible to define in the general floor plan.

an Exterior space in the dimensioned sketch

Interior patio of the Joan Miró Foundation, Barcelona, Spain, by Josep Lluis Sert.

The patio of the Centre d'Estudis d'Art Contemporani (Center of Contemporary Art Studies) of the Joan Miró Foundation in Barcelona, Spain, work of Josep Lluis Sert completed in 1975, is the theme chosen for describing an exterior space by means of a dimensioned sketch. This patio is the center around which different exhibit halls are developed and assembled; they open onto it, so it becomes a spatial and visual connection between them.

On considering this exterior, one should keep in mind that interest should be centered on the plans that define it—that is, the floor plan, with the different textures of the elements that compose it, and the four facades that enclose it—without including more interior construction details.

PROCESS OF ELABORATION

The first step is to confirm that the floor plan is a square of about 15 m (49 ft) per side. If the sketch described a smaller surface, the views could be arranged by unfolding the facades around the plan at the center. However, the dimensions here require that the initial sketch be complemented by other, larger drawings that would not fit on a manageable size of paper.

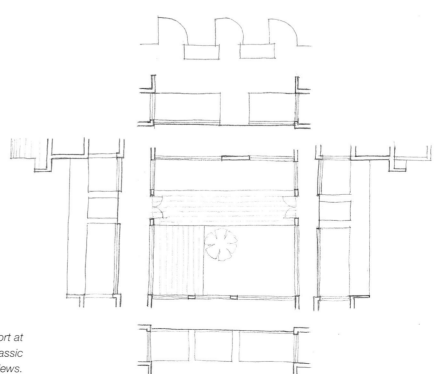

General pencil sketch. First effort at drawing the subject with a classic arrangement of views.

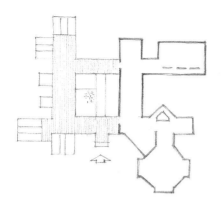

Reference sketch in pencil showing the interior patio of the Museum.

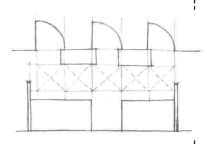

The geometric compositional strategy analyzed in this example is not so evident in other cases. There are times when the architectural element being analyzed may not have been composed in a geometric manner. Therefore, one should not be unduly determined in looking for it.

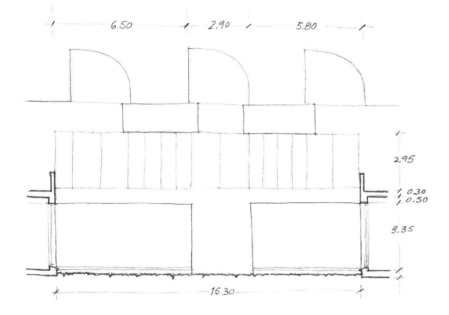

6.50   2.90   5.80

2.95

0.30
0.50

3.35

15.30

Larger pencil sketch used to provide more detail in the plan and the principal elevation of the exterior space.

The drawing begins with the basic square where the different areas of pavement and of vegetation are located. A thickness is assigned to the walls that surround the planting, noting the solid parts and the openings. Each elevation is projected in its designated direction, laying out the heights by proportion and defining the openings, the walls, and the cantilevers already laid out on the plan.

Once three of the sides, despite their complexity, are sufficiently defined for this initial drawing, the fourth and most emblematic side is added as precisely as the size of the drawing will permit. Given the importance of this fourth side, its geometry is analyzed, noticing in it a modular compositional strategy, evident in the recessed joints that can be seen in the wall that will help to proportion and lay out the sketch. This compositional strategy is transferred to a larger sketch where all of it can be displayed, including the placement of the windows in the sectioned areas. On the plan that corresponds to this elevation, the pavement and the vegetation are detailed, and greater definition is given to the walls, doors, and windows.

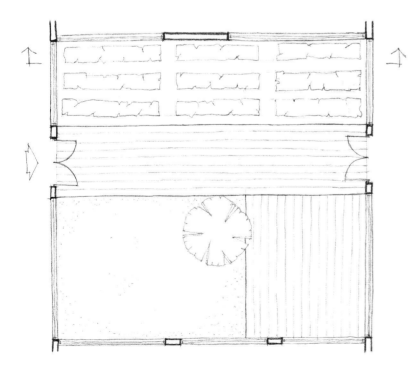

the selected project is a traditional house in the historic center of Sant Marti Vell, a municipality close to Girona and Figueres, Spain, very near to Púbol, where Salvador Dalí lived until his death. In this geographic setting, the urban nucleus has been entirely restored thanks to the efforts of Elsa Peretti, a Tiffany designer and creator of the foundation that owns many of the houses in the town.

a dimensioned Sketch
of traditional architecture

The nucleus of Sant Marti is very small (barely 15 houses in all) and lies clustered around a church dating from the mid-sixteenth century, on a small hill. The bell towers of the neighboring municipalities can be seen just a few miles away, as is characteristic of the region. The majority of the structures are agricultural in nature and they have been transformed over the centuries as uses and customs have changed. By the early 1950s, they had been virtually abandoned. Soon after, Elsa Peretti initiated her efforts at restoration, with the goal of creating a space for her studio, a residence, and a small museum, similar to what Salvador Dalí had accomplished in the neighboring town of Púbol, and what other professionals and creative people were doing in the surrounding areas.

Interior of this traditional house.

Pencil dimensioned sketch showing the whole area to be studied, with heavier lines indicating the house.

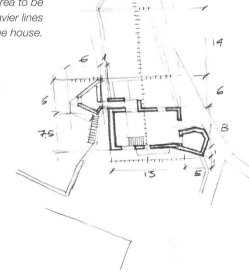

The ensemble seen from the plaza.

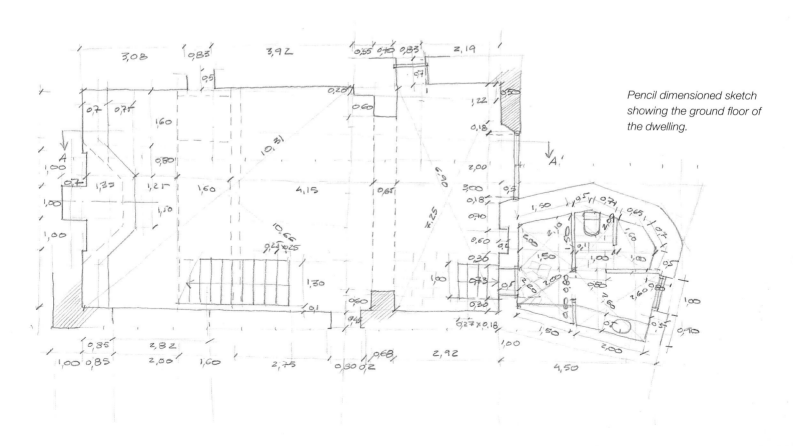

Pencil dimensioned sketch showing the second floor of the dwelling.

DESCRIPTION OF THE TASK

In this context, the idea was to restore and reuse the different houses, with the condition that original materials, ideally antique, be used whenever possible. In the process, the existing spaces would be transformed to serve modern demands. This is how two antique haylofts and a house in ruins were joined to create the Casa Gran (the Great House), and its patios became a gathering place for all of the guests of the Foundation.

Later, a tower was erected from scratch on the site where a fortified house had once stood. It was built following a composite sculptural strategy that, while not typical, uses traditional materials. The tower provides a lookout point from which people can observe the whole region, and it also serves as a means of repairing the ruined profile of the town, with its sunken roofs. A bridge similar to other existing elevated passages that connect the different houses of the town was built to join the tower to Casa Gran.

Thus, the ensemble combines the characteristics of traditional architectural endeavor with restoration and expansion projects. These are the essential motivations for the creation of the different dimensioned sketches.

Pencil dimensioned sketch showing the ground floor of the dwelling.

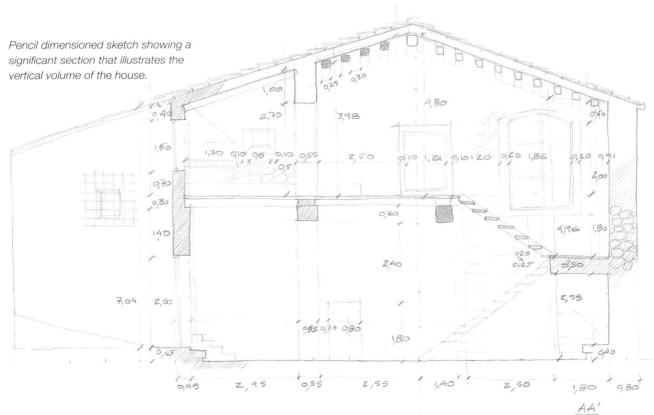

WORK STRATEGY

In historic restorations, nothing should be taken for granted. The thickness, angle, and inclination of the walls can vary. The floor is probably not level. And the existing spaces more than likely evolved through an accumulation of spontaneous adaptations to the site, not from a directed plan.

Furthermore, next to walls of rubble or rocks or other humble materials, fragments of masonry and decorations of historic value may appear.

Given these characteristics, the first step is to look the site over entirely, inside and out, and, if possible, observe it from above in order to get an idea of the ensemble and its volume. In this particular case, we went up the bell tower of the church, but failing such a vantage point, a general plan from the municipality or an aerial photograph can provide the same information.

Next we must establish a path or axis of the outline and take measurements by laying down a pattern of paces or using a long measuring tape. Beginning with the entrance, this path should lead through all of the rooms in straight lines that turn at right angles. From these angles emerge, like branches, other paths that lead to points of interest. In this way the ensemble is laid out and the proportions of the interior and exterior spaces are defined.

Pencil dimensioned sketch of the plan and elevation of a newly incorporated chimney.

Pencil dimensioned sketch showing a significant section that illustrates the vertical volume of the house.

Concentrating on the principal room and starting with an initial grid-outline, other paths, whose origin is marked on the ground perpendicular to the first, extend out to the walls. These lines define the width and orientation of the different walls and their irregularities. This first intuitive assessment provides a framework for the sketch on the paper, with margins left for dimensions and annotations.

At this point, more and more detail is added. First, the interior enclosures are profiled, and then the complementary elements.

Given the complexity of this particular site, it was decided to draw the plan on one sheet and the interior elevations or sections on others. Therefore, the layout lines extend to the edges in order to continue these points on other sheets. Slowly, the details are defined, moving from the general to the specific, finishing with the dimensions, along the grid lines or other similar lines. The diagonals are also measured at this point in order to establish the orientations of the walls, since this data will later inform the scale plans.

Pencil dimensioned sketch of the plan and section of the main door.

Pencil dimensioned sketch of the main facade, which looks out on the plaza.

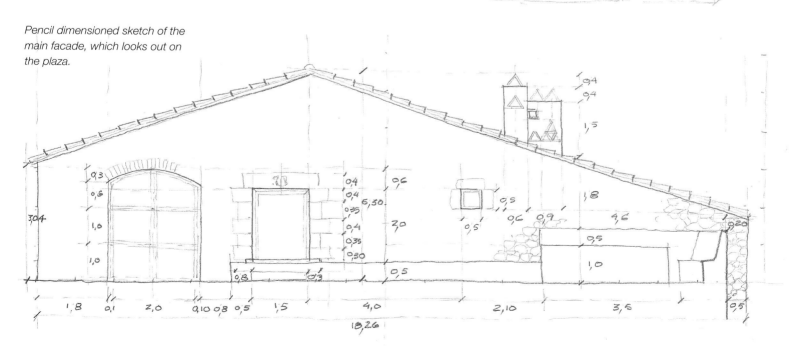

The new tower built with traditional materials of the region.

Pencil dimensioned sketch of the ensemble being studied. The shaded section indicates a detail of the tower.

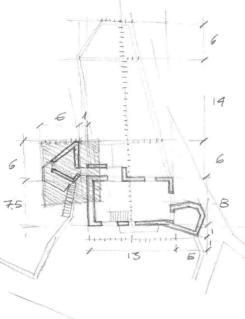

MORE DETAILS TO CONSIDER

Another important aspect to keep in mind is that the thickness of the walls is unknown. For this reason, the axes of the outline should pass through the doors that connect the rooms and end at windows that allow for measuring the thickness, or follow vertical openings and stairways in order to detect the thicknesses of the ceilings as well as any tilt. However, it is necessary to simplify the process a little, since an exhaustive survey of the building would require techniques of topography and aerial photography that are very expensive and not always justified, particularly if they will not help with the walls.

On this page is a selection of different dimensioned sketches showing the ensemble and the house. They provide examples of all the techniques for recording data described previously, and of the common graphic range of endeavors like this that include floor plans, sections or interior elevations, exterior elevations, construction and decorative details, and the site plan.

We chose as illustrative details one of the building's noble doors, preserved in the process of restoration, and one of the new chimneys, constructed with traditional materials in a modern expressionist design.

Pencil dimensioned sketches of the ground and second floors.

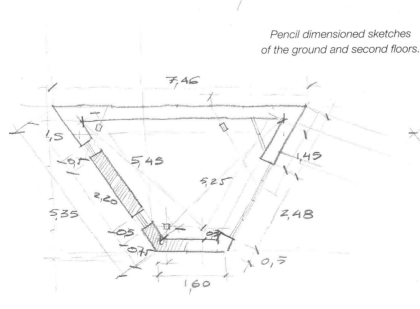

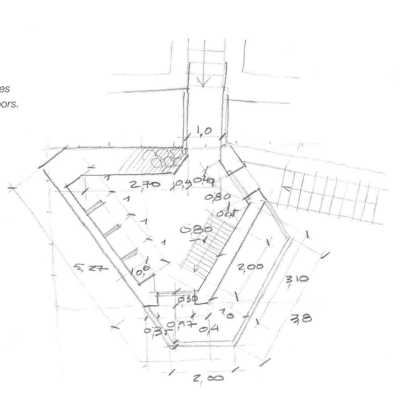

DIMENSIONED SKETCH OF A MULTISTORY SPACE

As in other examples of the dimensioned sketch, this one begins by marking the paper to divide it into as many units as there are paces or extent in the space to be drawn, leaving room to indicate the dimensions. These points and axes are drawn with very light lines, for example with a 2H lead. In the second step, the walls are drawn, or rather, the envelope or outline of the space and its subdivisions are drawn, also with very fine lines that extend to the edge of the paper so further projections can be drawn on other sheets of paper.

On this base, the walls are drawn; their thickness, if it is known, is indicated very lightly for the moment. Only when all the pieces are joined together do we trace over the line with a softer lead, B or the like, in order to differentiate the section from the projection.

This distribution of the walls, edges, changes of level, and floors with different thicknesses can then be completed with textures. Be careful not to create confusion; follow clear criteria and assign linear weights according to the importance of the item that is represented.

Finally, the dimension lines are drawn lightly. Make sure to group them at the sides, and letter the dimensions and mark the ends clearly.

*Pencil dimensioned sketch
of an elevation of the tower.*

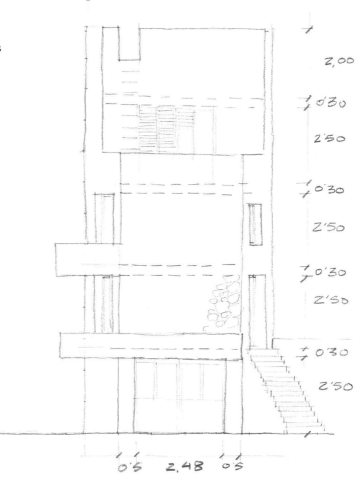

*Pencil dimensioned sketches of the third and
fourth floors.*

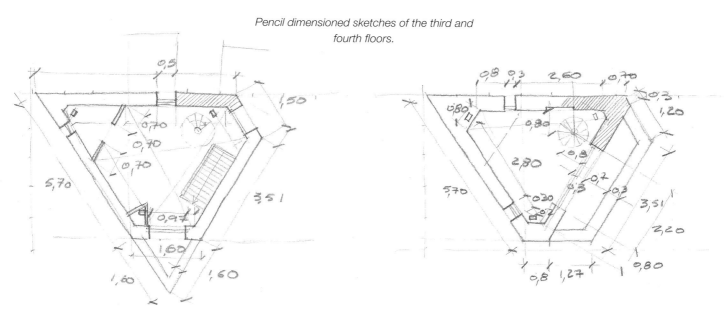

the Idea sketch.

Analysis of architectural forms

"THE DRAWING IS THE FIRST CONSTRUCTION IN ARCHITECTURE. THE ARCHITECT, WHEN DRAWING, IS ALREADY CONSTRUCTING (IN THE STRICTEST, MOST IMMEDIATE, AND ACCEPTED SENSE OF THE WORD) THE ARCHITECTURAL STRUCTURE."

J. A. Cortes and J. R. Moneo. Comentarios sobre dibujos de 20 arquitectos actuales (Comments on drawings by 20 current architects), 1976.

architectural

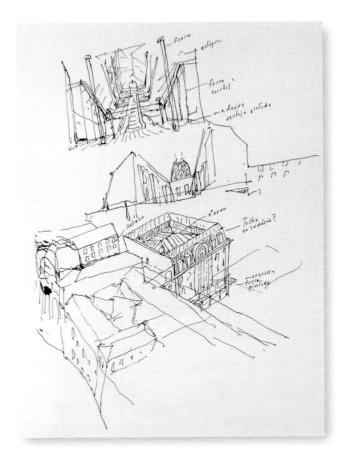

ALVARO SIZA.
REHABILITATION PROJECT FOR THE GRADELLA BUILDING, LISBON, PORTUGAL.
INK IDEA SKETCH.

Views.

When envisioning an architectural design, the drawing

becomes a basic tool in the process of conception, as a means of communicating the concept to others, simulating the reality not yet built.

It is essential, therefore, to master the systems of representation that facilitate this simulation, just as one should know how to create views or axonometric and one-point perspectives of a given project, since these representations show the volumetric appearance of the architectural form.

Thus, the idea sketch, a quickly executed freehand drawing, serves to focus the attention of the architect. It defines the geometric characteristics of the architectural form, starting with its outlines. In order to create the idea sketch, we use the conventional systems of representation, ranging from simple line to hatching and shading, with particular emphasis on the suggestion of volume and depth through the use of shadows.

Fundamentals of linear perspective

the linear perspective system of representation is based on the principle that an element is projected onto a plane in a convergent, not orthogonal, manner. Visual rays radiate from a given point of view, or station point, where the observer is located, and end at each one of vertices of the element, thus generating a pyramid (P.V.-ABCD).

BASIC PRINCIPLES

This method is very effective in representing the real view of a model if we close one eye and do not move. However, that is not a realistic vision of the model, but rather a linear or flat simplification, since we focus with two eyes that we move in order to understand what lies in front of us.

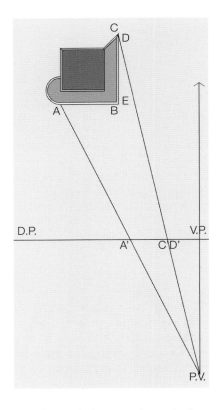

Observe how the drawing plane is perpendicular to the visual axis of the spectator.

Axonometric diagram of the frontal (one-point) perspective projection. This example is the Gwathmey Studio, Amagansett, New York, by Charles Gwathmey. Throughout this series of drawings we will use the following symbols:
P.V., point of view or station point (position of the observer);
D.P., drawing plane or picture plane (the paper); V.P., vanishing point;
H.L., horizon line (at eye level).

This view results from projecting the scene onto the drawing plane (the paper). The straight line A'B' is projected horizontally on the drawing and the perpendicular lines B'C' or E'D' converge to the same vanishing point, V.P.

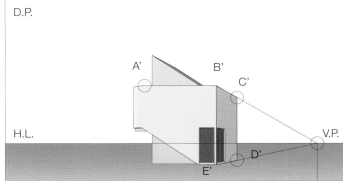

Using as a base a plan and elevation of the Gwathmey House, we construct a one-point perspective, applying the process to the model. The vertical lines passing through A and C, which coincide with the drawing plane, are drawn the same size. The horizontal lines, for example AB, which pass through the end points of those vertical lines and are perpendicular to the plane, converge at point V.P., always located on the horizon line.

The intersection of the visual pyramid with a vertical plane, that of the paper, generates a flat representation of the volume similar to the picture seen on a movie screen. The different calculations are made with views of the model in orthographic projection (plan and elevation).

In the diagram the observer is located at ground level, defined by a horizontal plane called the geometric plane or ground plane. The eyes of the observer lie above this plane on another horizontal plane, the horizon plane (at height h), which cuts the drawing plane (D.P.) and defines the horizon line (H.L.). The perpendicular projection over the H.L. of the point of view (P.V.) generates the center of vision (C.V.), and the distance between this and the point of view (P.V.) defines the central axis of vision. The angle formed by the visual rays, which start at the observer and end at the farthest vertices of the model, is called the angle of vision. This angle should lie between 40° and 60°.

Linear perspectives can be frontal and oblique or angled. In frontal one-point perspectives, the drawing plane is arranged parallel to the sides that are emphasized; any vertical or horizontal line is projected as is onto the drawing plane (D.P.). In oblique or two-point perspectives, the drawing plane lies in any vertical orientation (not parallel) with respect to the model.

ONE-POINT (FRONTAL) PERSPECTIVE

Keeping earlier discussions in mind, an exterior wall that is frontally placed is projected onto the drawing by means of lines that define a similar form. Any other wall parallel to the first is projected in greater or lesser size depending on its position relative to the first wall, but maintaining its proportions. The edges perpendicular to the wall converge at the center of vision (C.O.V.), which coincides here with the vanishing point (V.P.), unlike what occurs with the oblique (two-point) perspective.

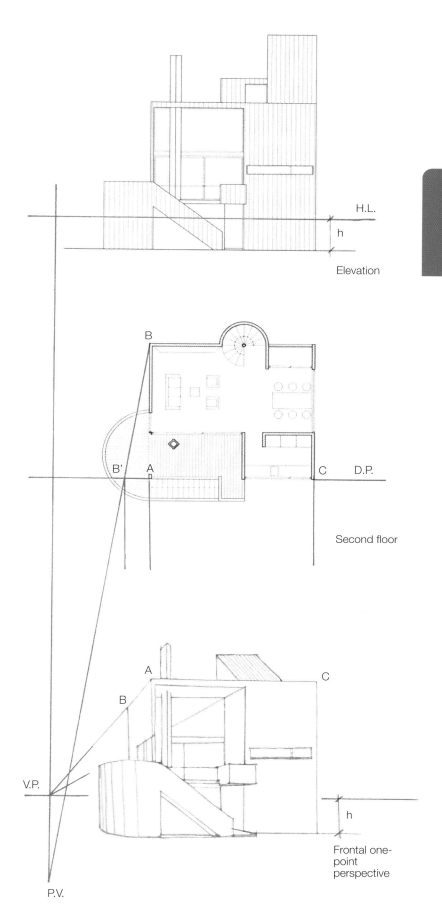

H.L.

h

Elevation

B

B' A   C   D.P.

Second floor

A   C

B

V.P.

h

Frontal one-point perspective

P.V.

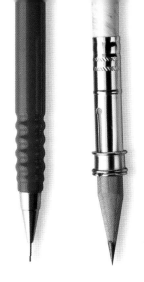

If a section of the residence is drawn along a given plane C-C' and that plane is used as the drawing plane, one can obtain a section perspective by applying the described concepts.

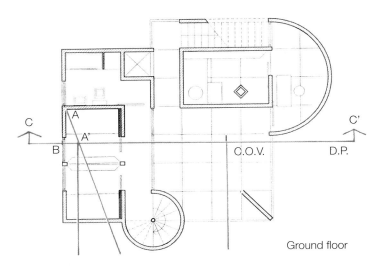

Ground floor

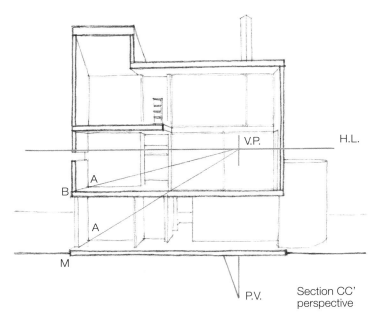

Section CC'
perspective

If the drawing plane is arranged to coincide with one of the vertical edges of the previous model, its projection is of identical size. On this edge, the measuring line (M.L.), the height of the observer, or any other measurement can be defined to the same scale.

A very common variation of frontal one-point perspective in architecture is the perspective section. In this case, the drawing plane is placed to coincide with a given section. The result is a drawing that is not intended to show a real view of the model, but rather to enrich the section by incorporating the depth of the surroundings. The point of view may be in an unlikely place—for example, at mid-height and farther away than the building itself.

OBLIQUE (TWO-POINT) PERSPECTIVE

The principal difference between the oblique (or two-point) perspective and the frontal (one-point) perspective is that all the lines other than the vertical ones are converging lines. With the model placed in front of the observer, the view of the model offers different orientations for each of its sides, which presumably are perpendicular to each other, for the sake of simplicity. Normally, none of them exhibits excessive foreshortening, so the view appears as real as possible. A 30°/60° orientation is acceptable, but given that this is a freehand sketch drawn on a previously prepared graphic, any approximation is valid as long as neither of the two sides is seen in a very frontal way.

Elevations and sections of the two remaining floors as complementary graphic documentation to understand the architect's own house. Charles Gwathmey, Amagansett, New York.

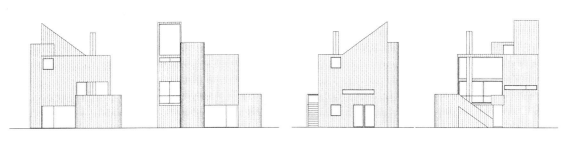

Third floor

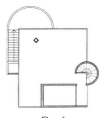

Roof

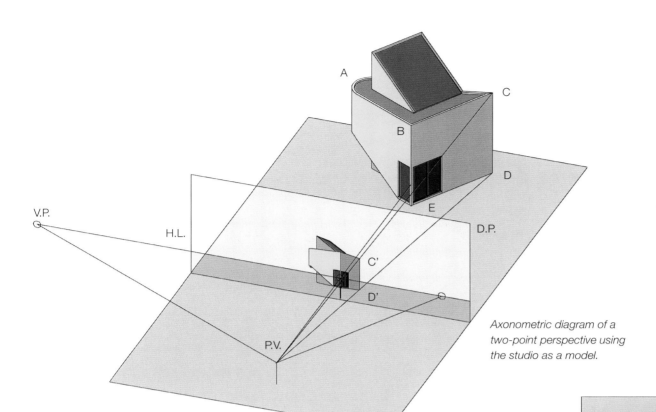

An axonometric model has been used to explain the process of construction of a two-point perspective, but in practice the perspective should be based on the plan, elevations, and sections.

Axonometric diagram of a two-point perspective using the studio as a model.

If we focus on its projection on the floor plan, we see how the vanishing points (V.P.) of the different directions can be obtained by drawing a line passing through the viewpoint of the observer (P.V.) that is parallel to each of the general orientations (AB and ED). You can see, thus, that these points do not coincide with the center of vision, which is the case with frontal one-point perspective. The points where these straight lines cut the drawing plane along the horizon line (H.L.) define the vanishing points (V.P.), which are then marked. Their distance to the center of vision is measured and these values are transferred to the layout, projecting the relative position of the vertical edges that define the envelope of the element (B'E', C'D'. . .). In any model it is possible to detect other families or orientations of straight lines that are horizontal and parallel. Each one of them converges on a vanishing point found on the horizon line and is obtained graphically with the techniques already described.

Once the vertical edges have been projected and the height of the observer chosen, lines B'C', B'A', E'D', . . . are drawn from the measuring line (the line that coincides with the drawing plane). These lines converge to the different points that then cut the verticals defining the volume.

The vanishing points are obtained by drawing lines parallel to the sides, starting at the observer, until they cut through the horizon line.

This is the result of projecting the scene onto the drawing plane using two-point perspective.

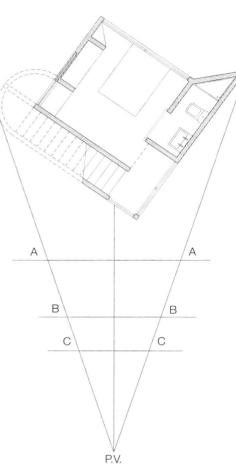

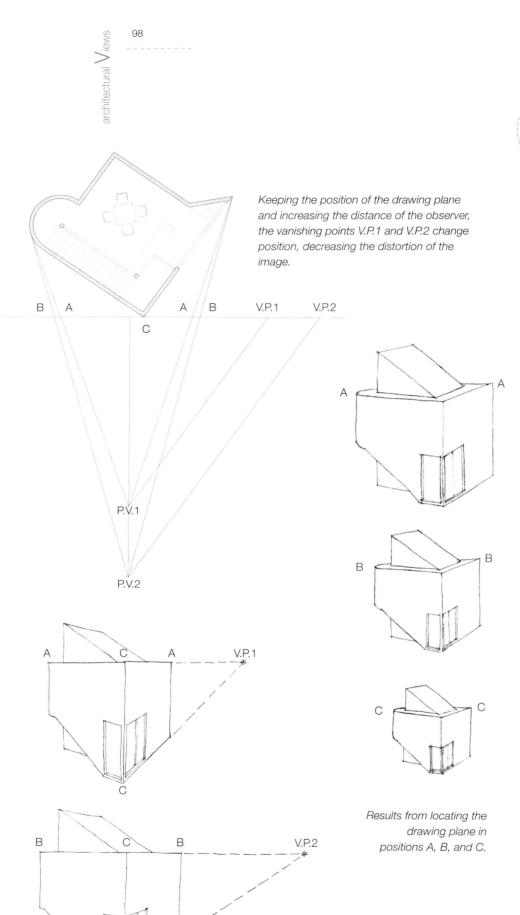

Keeping the position of the drawing plane and increasing the distance of the observer, the vanishing points V.P.1 and V.P.2 change position, decreasing the distortion of the image.

Results from locating the drawing plane in positions A, B, and C.

Results from P.V.1 and P.V.2.

Keeping the position of the observer and the model and varying the drawing plane, similar projections of different sizes are obtained.

CHANGES IN DISTANCE BETWEEN THE OBSERVER AND THE MODEL

The distance between the observer and the subject of a linear perspective depends largely on the size of the model and whether or not it should appear entirely in a single view. Keeping the drawing plane in the same place, at a greater distance from the viewpoint, the drawing will be slightly larger, and vice versa. This becomes more evident when the position of the drawing plane is changed. Although it can be placed farther away, the drawing plane generally lies between the observer and the model, in which case the view is more distorted the closer the model is to the observer, and becomes increasingly flattened as the observer moves away.

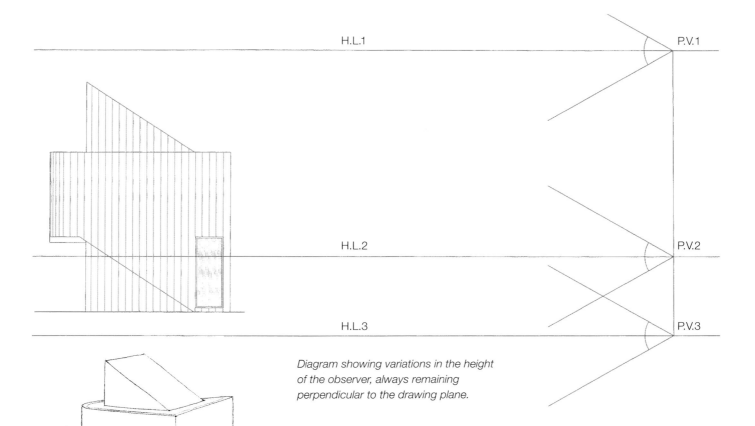

H.L.1   P.V.1

H.L.2   P.V.2

H.L.3   P.V.3

*Diagram showing variations in the height
of the observer, always remaining
perpendicular to the drawing plane.*

From P.V.1

From P.V.2

CHANGES IN THE HEIGHT OF THE VIEWPOINT

Once the perspective layout of the building has been established from a normal eye level, you can see, using the same base, how its appearance would change by varying the height of the viewpoint or of the observer. These atypical views, in other words, neither common nor accessible, are usually executed when, for example, the designer wants to show the whole ensemble of a building and its distant surroundings. This is the case with an aerial or bird's-eye view. If, on the other hand, the designer wishes to show the structure and the detail of a ceiling, a worm's-eye view should be used. By not varying the position of the observer with respect to the drawing, the relative position of the different edges will be valid with respect to the center of vision. However, their height will change in relation to the horizon line. Therefore, from an elevated view, the heights of things and the points at which the edges of the building meet the ground plane will be measured from the horizon line downward, since it is the line that passes through the eyes of the observer, who is located well above the building.

The opposite occurs with a view at floor level or below (worm's-eye view), where the base of the layout is the same, but the vertices of the edges are measured from the horizon line upward.

*Linear (two-point) perspectives resulting from the three
different heights of the horizon line in the top diagram.*

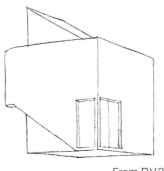

From P.V.3

layout and Measuring
of architectural forms

every model can be defined according to a minimal enveloping outline based on a simple geometric figure: cube, cylinder, prism, pyramid, etc. It is then subdivided and the definitive volume approximated using other similar geometric figures, submultiples of the first.

GEOMETRIC AND GRAPHIC LAYOUT
The analogy is that of a packing box for merchandise, the protective filling for the intermediate spaces, and the product.

This is the strategy used to create a layout for the rough designs of a building and the elements that compose it, executed in axonometric and linear perspective.

We begin with the axonometric, because with this perspective the distances can be measured all along their axes and because, as single distant views, it permits a complete description of the model with economy of graphic means.

With this strategy, even in very extensive buildings or those with organic forms, the volume can be described in a rational way, in an initial exercise of architectural analysis that illustrates how an architectural work can be composed.

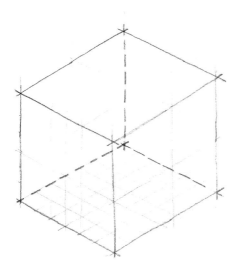

A simple axonometric prism is converted into a basic "container" for a building, in this case, the Gwathmey residence.

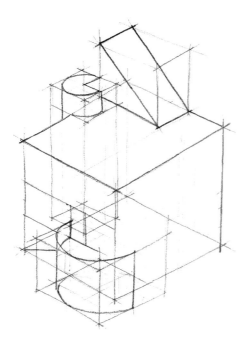

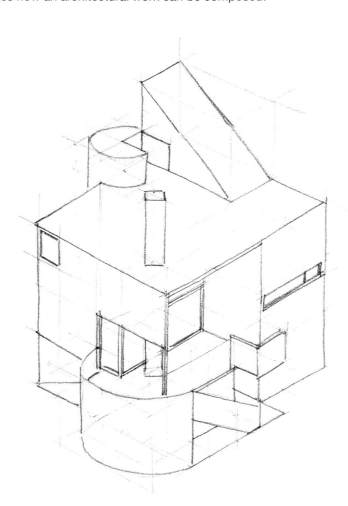

The prism is progressively subdivided according to the volumetric elements that compose this architectural form.

Finally, the windows, stairs, and those elements that define the analyzed subject are added.

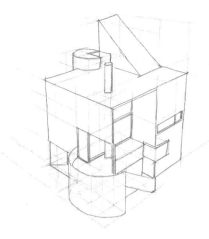

When establishing a layout for the same subject in one-point perspective, it is important to be aware that the initial volume and its divisions should converge.

LAYOUT AND MEASUREMENT IN ONE-POINT PERSPECTIVE

We have seen how any line situated in the drawing plane presents real measurements, or measurements to scale, depending on the base model. This quality can be advantageous in the one-point perspective system for marking a similar vertical or horizontal line, measurement lines that then generate a set of lines that transfer these values to any depth of the perspective space.

A somewhat different task involves representing depth in a way parallel to the drawing plane. Here various strategies can be used. We will focus on those in common use in the freehand idea sketch.

SIMPLIFIED METHODS

The first method is based on the premise that every time the distance between the ground plane and the plane of the horizon is divided by two, the represented depth doubles. Obviously, if you know the position and the height of the observer as well as the location of the drawing plane, the rest is easy. The second method involves the application of Thales' theorem, the perspectival theorem of Thales. A ruler (or graphic scale) is made over a horizontal line that arises from the lowest point of the line of vertical measure (M.L.). This mark is based on the same units of height (h). The depth of the space is known from the plan; it is enough to mark this value to scale on the straight line of horizontal measure (M.L.) and join its end to the point of intersection of the ground with the rear exterior wall.

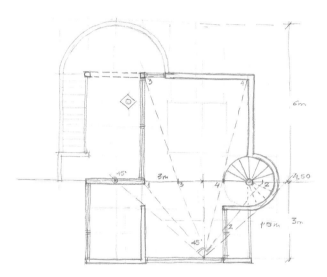

The drawing plane is located on the plan, and edge 1 coincides with it, as does edge 2, which defines the angle of vision. Then edges 3 and 4 are projected, thus defining the scenic box.

A ruler or a graphic scale can be defined using the edges located in the drawing plane.

If one measures in the plan diagram the distance between the observer and the drawing plane and places that distance in the perspective layout, it can be checked that when one divides in two the distance between the horizon line and the ground, the depth represented is doubled.

In order to subdivide the space in depth, one can also apply Thales' theorem, according to which it is possible to divide in proportional parts two segments united at one end by drawing lines parallel to the line that unites their other two ends.

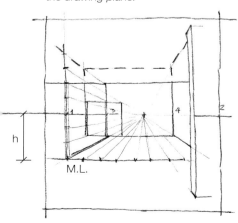

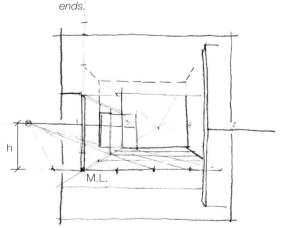

The third method uses the representation in perspective of a square whose height extends from the floor to the horizon line represented on the lateral wall so that if one joins a vertex with the midpoint of the opposite side, another square is created, and so on, successively generating new squares in perspective. The problem lies in defining the first square. If we are not very sure of our visual ability, we can make use of the distance points that are the vanishing points of all the straight horizontal lines that form 45° angles with the square. In order to draw these lines, the distance between the observer and the drawing plane is transferred to the right or left of the center of vision. If a straight horizontal frontal line is drawn to the foot of the vertical measuring line and its end is joined with the distance point, this will provide the same value in depth.

COMBINATION OF STRATEGIES

Based on this grid, a framework can be designed for any geometric figure: stairs, roofs, circular forms, etc. In the case of stairs, the perspectival theorem of Thales is applied to the ground as well as the vertical in order to define the number of steps and their heights, producing a grid that facilitates the drawing.

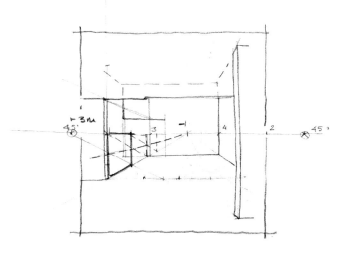

In order to define the first square it is necessary to return to the ground plan and draw lines from the observer at 45° angles, so that the distance between the observer and the drawing plane is the same as the distance between the center of vision (always in the center of the perspective) and the point where these lines cut across the horizon.

This interior one-point perspective of the sitting room in the Gwathmey House is an example of the application of the concepts discussed here.

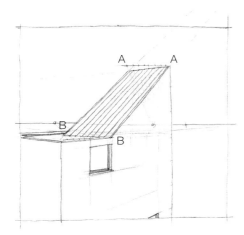

Resolution of the convergence of the roof of the house.

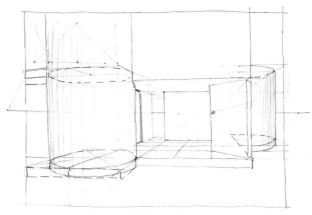

Layout and definition of the idea sketch in one-point perspective showing the circular forms on the ground floor.

Calculations that must be done in order to define the stairway in linear perspective.

Thales' theorem can be used for the roof as well to generate the ridge A-A and the lower line B-B. Once divided in equal parts, the equivalent points can be joined two by two, checking to see that they converge toward a point situated above the horizon line. In the case of circular forms, an earlier layout acts as a base that is then transferred to the perspective. Complete circles are not seen as round, but rather as ellipses. It is therefore better to put the circumscribing square in perspective, placing in it the figure's different points of intersection and indicating the apparent contours. The rest is drawn freehand, maintaining the tangencies.

Exterior view of the ensemble in oblique perspective. The different walls are shaded in order to reinforce the sense of depth.

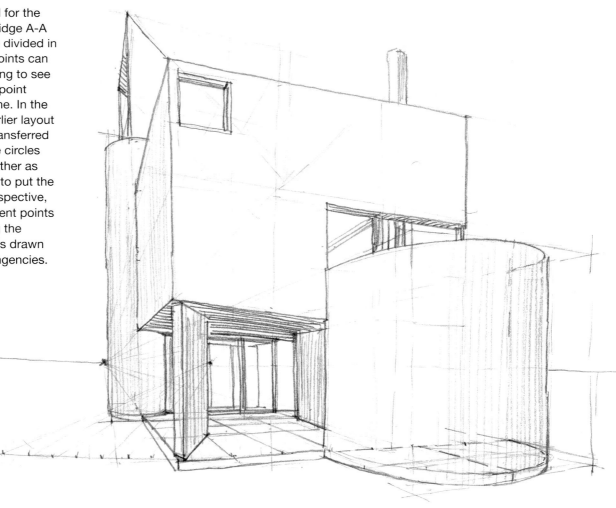

Once the theoretical foundations of one-point perspective are known, it is necessary to select the point of view and layout that best describe the building. For that, we will take a mental stroll around the building, an itinerant visit to choose the most suitable views for describing it.

layout and Choice of views

METHOD OF APPROACH

With the plan of a project established, as well as the appearance of the section and elevations, the next step is to decide how an interior or exterior view will look: what will lie beyond the porch, whether the columns will hide the wall in the background, and so on. Imagine an observer who shines a flashlight whose beam, the angle of vision, illuminates the scene—this is known as the flashlight method. The observer tests whether the light passes between the different elements or illuminates everything at different distances, or if it is necessary to move toward the sides in order to better frame the scene.

Plans and elevations to become familiar with the Turegano House, Madrid, Spain, by Manuel Campo Baeza.

Then the overall size of the drawing should be determined; although the techniques of reproduction allow enlarging, this is not always easy when dealing with a freehand idea sketch. Cutting the drawing plane with the beam of a flashlight suffices to establish the relative size of the perspective.

We begin by trying some exterior views of the building, choosing different points of view seen from a straight standing position.

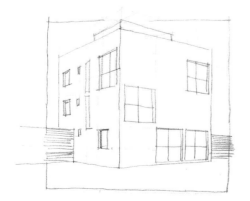

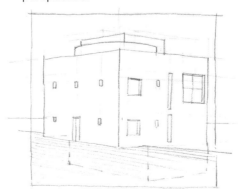

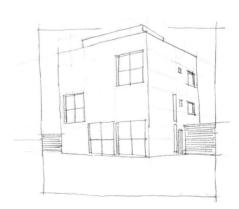

Finally, one must consider the height at which the observer sees the building. For a realistic and credible view, a coherent position and height are chosen for the observer. For a general image, an aerial view is chosen, but always within the cone of vision. Otherwise, the observer would be obliged to look down, meaning that the drawing plane would not be vertical, resulting in a plummeting view with three vanishing points—geometrically possible, but perceptually disagreeable and more difficult to draw.

Another option would be a section perspective or an external view eliminating some of the facades, depending on the model being considered and the understanding of that model. It is important to remember that in these projections many construction elements and interior views appear that may not be of interest. The trials, which an expert can skip, are absolutely necessary for someone who is just learning about perspective, because a bad layout can spoil the results. Consequently, a series of vignettes emerges from which the most deliberate and helpful examples are selected.

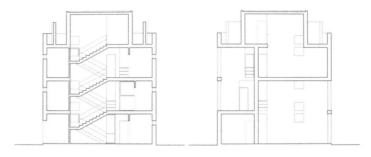

Complementary sections to enhance understanding of the Turegano House.

Once the most interesting views have been selected, variations in the treatment of materials or details can be introduced with tracing paper.

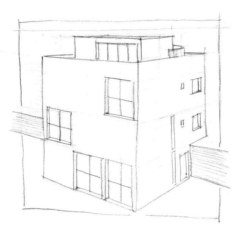

The review is completed with the creation of some partial views that are relevant to or of interest for understanding the work.

After an initial trial, views are chosen from among the most significant and the most descriptive views of the building.

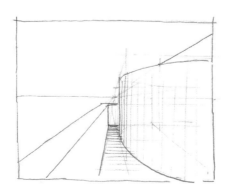

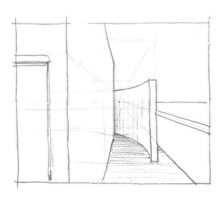

Sketching shadows. Basic concepts

as we saw in the section entitled "Shading: The Perception of Light," in the first chapter, the shadow is a fundamental feature in suggesting depth and volume in any drawing. The architectural idea sketch is no exception. Although it is an approximation executed freehand, the shadows must respond to lines and laws of geometry, intuitively interpreted.

GRAPHIC CONVENTION

The shadows discussed here are those created by the sun. This very distant source of light produces parallel rays of light. In idea sketches, the orientation of the sun generates shadows that move away from the observer, in order to avoid backlight, with an extension similar to the length of the edge AO or the plane that produces it (AOB). The underlying objective is to enhance the volume of the representation, rather than to achieve realism. In general, a graphic convention is adopted here placing the sun in the upper left part of the paper, generating shadows with an inclination and orientation of about 45°.

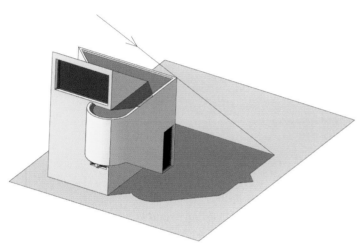

This axonometric diagram shows how shades are generated and cast by one object onto another.

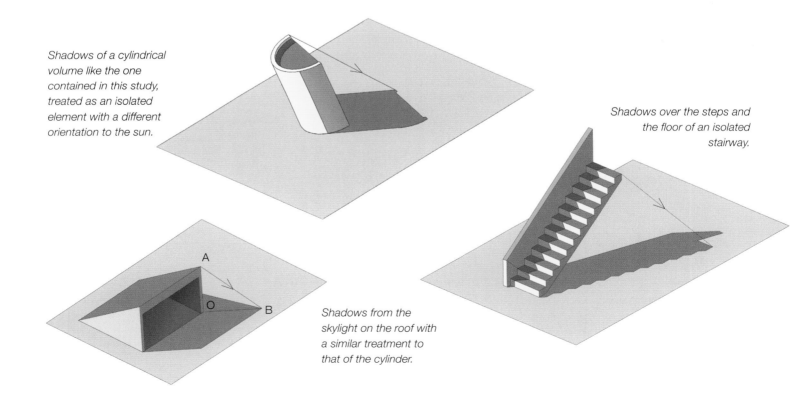

Shadows of a cylindrical volume like the one contained in this study, treated as an isolated element with a different orientation to the sun.

Shadows over the steps and the floor of an isolated stairway.

Shadows from the skylight on the roof with a similar treatment to that of the cylinder.

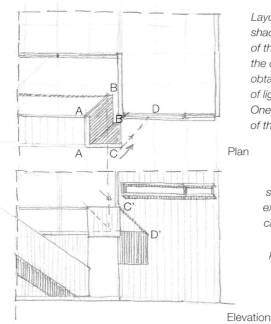

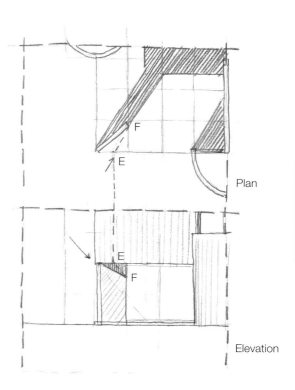

Layout showing the plan and elevation of the shadows cast by the balcony and elements of the residence. The point of projection from the corner of the balcony (C and C') is obtained by following the direction of the ray of light in the plan and elevation (D and D'). One proceeds in a similar way with the rest of the points.

Plan

Layout of the plan and elevation of the shadows cast by the roof and the inclined exterior wall of the ground floor. In order to calculate point F, where the shadow of the roof stops casting itself on the wall and passes to the ground, we define it on the plan. It is point E, where the ray becomes tangent.

Plan

Elevation

Elevation

In order to facilitate drawing the shadow, a general representation with preliminary dimensions is created for the plan and elevation, then the result is transferred to one-point perspective and adjusted by eye.

This is applied to models and complex architectural forms that can be simplified to other more elementary forms, keeping in mind that frequently the cast shadows of one body will overlap the shades of another, resulting in a single shadow for both.

Every flat horizontal surface (AA) casts a shadow over a plane (the ground) parallel to it, exactly equal to its perimeter (BB). When the plane (the wall) onto which the shadow is projected is perpendicular to it, the shadow's form is the result (C'D') of the intersection of the prism or cylinder of parallel rays which, originating in the dividing line of light/form shadow, will be cut by the plane where they are cast.

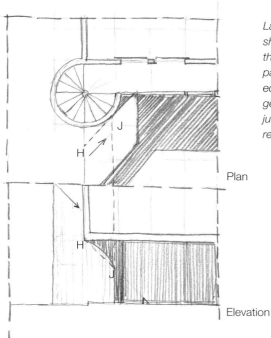

Layout showing the plan and elevation of the shadows cast by the roof and elements of the ground floor. The rays of the sun that pass along the horizontal edge of the roof's edge form a plane that cuts the cylinder, generating an ellipse (HJ) on the elevation, just like when a trunk is bevel-cut. For this reason, the shadow curves.

Plan

Elevation

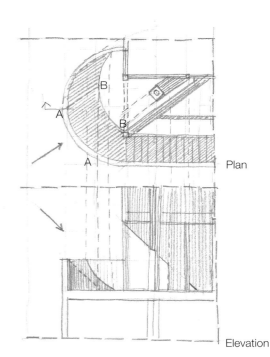

Layout showing the shadows on the second-floor terrace in the plan and elevation. The shadow from the circular banister onto the ground (BB) is equal and parallel to the border of the same shadow (AA).

Plan

Elevation

Shadows in orthographic projection

the sketching of shadows in orthogonal projections (plans, elevations, and sections) of architectural models stems from the need to suggest volume and depth. For this, their representation must be rigorous, even when done freehand, in order to avoid confusion.

SHADING OF ARCHITECTURAL ELEMENTS

The most common examples are elevations with shadows. In these, the idea is that any body protruding from another will cast its displaced shadow downward and to the right 1 m (3 ft). By applying the concepts previously explained, the shadows of more complex forms are resolved, as well as superimposition and transitions between different shadows.

The deeper the area of the facade, the more extensive the shadows will be.

Plans with shadows must suggest all the volume of the building, allowing choice between the exterior and the interior spaces, although the latter will probably hinder understanding of the distribution, which means that their design must be considered thoroughly from the start.

In a section, the common approach involves drawing the interior shadows of the volume, which result from cutting the building along a plane, while the exterior cast shadows will be the same for the whole volume. The interior shadows present a difficulty in that very deep spaces produce very dark areas that do not facilitate understanding of the drawing.

Shadows of the main facade of the residence.

Shadows cast by the walls of the ground floor. The shadows of the interior spaces have not been considered.

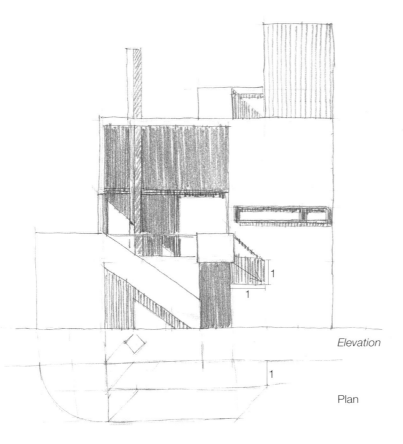

Elevation

Plan

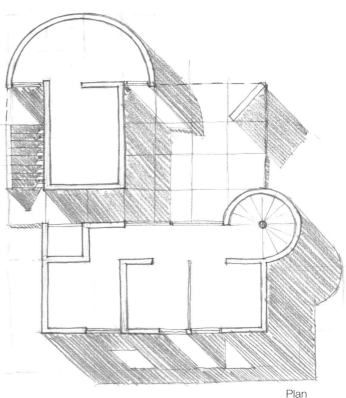

Plan

Idea sketch with shadows of the Sant Roc Market, Badalona, Spain, by Emili Donato.

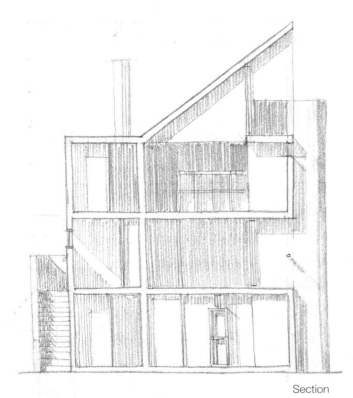

Section

Cast shadows on the section of the residence. The deepest spaces are totally shaded, distinguishing their elements with varying intensity.

Analysis of the shading of vegetation by applying the same principles.

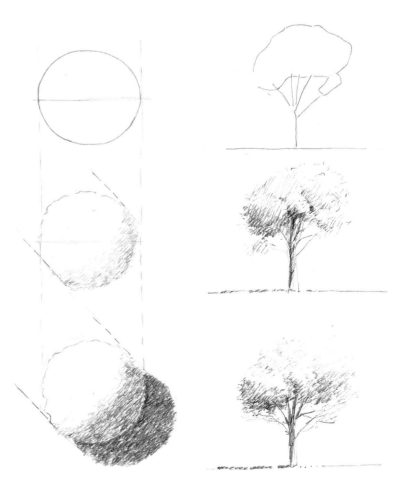

SHADING OF VEGETATION

When representing any form in perspective, almost at the same time that we define its contours, we feel the necessity to begin shading because this reinforces the perception of volume. Our theoretical base determines whether we do the shading in a more intuitive or a more rational way. Therefore, once the layout of the shadows of the architectural elements is understood, any other, no matter how organic, can be simplified as a series of framed geometric volumes, with shades and cast shadows calculated approximately, but coherently. The process is this: the dividing line between light and shadow is deduced, its shadow is projected, and its silhouette is reproduced.

Once one understands the scene, its volume and its shadows in axonometric projection as well as their freehand calculation in orthographic projection, it is time to deal with the problem of the calculation of shadows in a two-point perspective sketch.

Shadows
in linear perspective

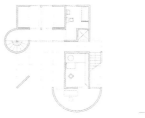

Ground floor and section of the residence. Basic documentation for the project.

PROPOSED METHOD

In the classic linear perspective system, if the sun is above the horizon, in front of the observer, a shadow results, directed toward the observer, producing a backlit image. If we want the shadow to fall away from us, as would be the logical and common circumstance, the method is very complex. A layout in linear perspective requires the vanishing point of the shadows to fall below the horizon, which is equivalent to having the sun behind the observer. Given that we are dealing with a freehand idea sketch, it is possible to simplify the method by calculating only the general shadows in the plan and the elevation, over a scale drawing that is then transferred to the linear perspective with the help of a supporting grid.

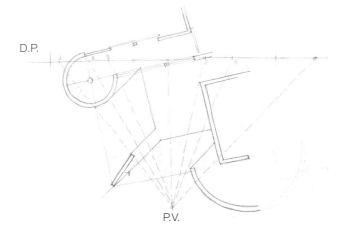

D.P.

P.V.

Plan diagram of the area to be shaded. The shadows and the layout of the linear perspective are calculated here.

Linear perspective with cast shadows on the porch based on the previous diagram. The points of the cast shadow on the pavement have been transferred, and the rest roughly calculated.

However, when trying to represent the shadows of an interior space, depending on its openings, it is also acceptable for these shadows to be directed toward the observer, since this reinforces the sensation of being in a covered and closed place.

In order to calculate the cast shadows of a building and its surroundings, the shadows should move away from the observer, linking the building to the setting that surrounds it. The shadows of projecting elements such as balconies and cornices help to add volume to the facades. The method is the same as described above. It can be completed with roughly calculated shadows of details or of lesser elements, applying the general theory of linear perspective. If, as in the example shown here, we make the sunlight cast shadows parallel to the drawing plane, the method is even simpler.

Plan and elevation of the residence. Calculation of the cast shadows and layout of the perspective.

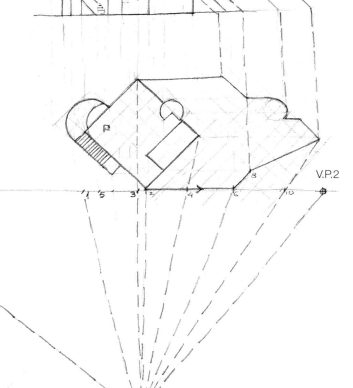

Linear perspective of the whole scene based on the previous diagram (see the corresponding numbered vertices). The rays of light have been chosen parallel to the drawing plane in order to simplify the process.

the Idea

ENRIC MIRALLES.
IDEA SKETCH SHOWING THE CONCEPT OF THE PROJECT FOR A SPORTS HALL IN
CHEMNITZ, GERMANY, WHERE THE LACK OF PRECISION IS SUGGESTIVE OF AN IDEA.

sketch
in architecture.
Now that the previous pages
have provided a brief description

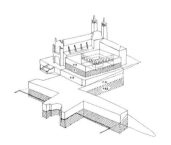

of the idea sketch, it is necessary to emphasize the importance that it possesses as a tool in the analysis and description of architecture. Since the focus of this book is to teach how to create these drawings, rigor is preferred and the time for execution will be longer than normal, between a half hour and an hour. When the shadows, textural attributes, materials, furnishings, atmosphere, and vegetation are adequately represented, the simulation of the future reality is much better. The idea sketch can be used by someone starting out in this discipline to analyze built architecture, but above all to conceive, study, and represent projects. In the first case, the shape of the architectural concept takes priority; in the second, the attempt to show the volumetric definition and its plastic appearance is the priority.

the creative idea Sketch.
from the mind to the paper

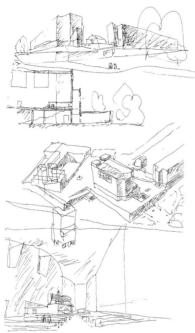

Idea sketches from the project for a church in Marco de Canavezes, Portugal, by Alvaro Siza. The designer combines diverse projections.

Idea sketches in one-point perspective for the Kansai-Kan Library, Kyoto, Japan, by Dominique Perrault. The human figures clarify the scale of the place.

t he idea sketch is used in the phase of creation in two ways: creation in a strict sense, and for the presentation of the project. The substantial difference between the two lies in the degree of polish and precision.

THE SUGGESTIVE LINE

When ideas flow to the mind of the person designing, they do so in a rush, which makes the idea sketch the ideal medium for shaping and testing. It is an imprecise drawing on which organizational diagrams are overlaid with structural criteria, corrections, and annotations in different projections. The idea sketch shapes an almost organic whole that gradually, in successive attempts, gains in precision. It is an intimate and personal work for the exclusive use of the designer, not always understandable to others. Once the idea is established, it should be adjusted with greater precision, in plans, elevations, sections, or in views of the project with materials, shadows, and figures, but without forgetting that, in the end, it is a technical drawing. The idea sketch thus becomes a work of communication, to be understood by others, which requires a rigorous approach.

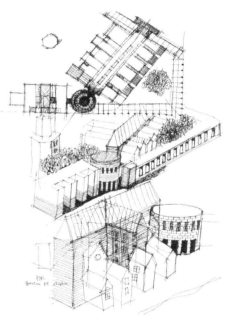

Idea sketches with different representations from various projects by Aldo Rossi.

Idea sketch in aerial one-point perspective for the Fine Art Museum of Houston, Texas, by Rafael Moneo. This example includes the different planes and landmarks of the city.

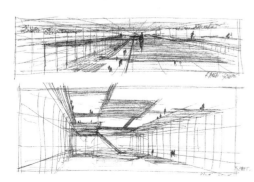

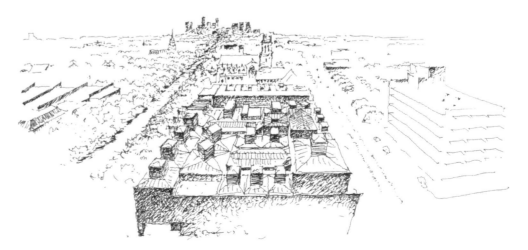

On other occasions, the idea sketch is intended to anticipate reality, simulating it with a more realistic or presentation-style drawing.

Examples of the first two types of idea sketch frequently represent works from different architects of recognized prestige and they are common practice in any study of architecture. The idea sketch used in presentations is more and more difficult to find given the rise of digital techniques. Idea sketches used in creation and those for communication constitute the schematic sketches that are used to analyze and describe built architecture. They are drawings that do not attempt to show the appearance of the buildings, since these can be visited, but rather try to describe aspects that are not immediately evident. They are rhetorical drawings that are directed to viewers versed in the material, the reason for which they are centered on particular aspects of the architecture, like its structure, organization, or the relationship between the parts. Idea sketches are thus schematic views, not realistic because they reflect concepts that are not perceptual and that will be tackled later.

Photograph manipulated with graphite and ink from the Vienna Expo of 1996 (competition) by Jean Nouvel. The realism of this idea sketch for presentation stems from the photographs on which it is based.

Pencil idea sketch of the CSH No. 13 House from 1946, by Richard Neutra. The designer emphasizes the pavement in order to describe the interior setting of the residence.

Watercolor-pencil idea sketch for the Berkowitz-Odgis House of 1983–1987 in Massachusetts, by Steven Holl. The dark texture of the vegetation and dunes brings the construction closer to the foreground.

idea sketch Analysis.
architectural description

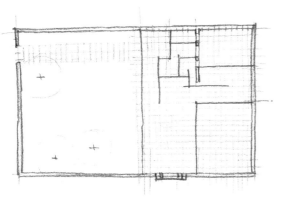

to analyze an architectural element is to describe its appearance and composition based on some commonly accepted systematic criteria. This process is accomplished in the graphic medium of the drawing, and the methodology employed consists of assessing the perceptual and architectural concepts in order to represent them. Drawing is an excellent medium for teaching. Incorporating a variety of theoretical concepts, it constitutes a common discipline in schools of architecture and design. Furthermore, drawing represents a basic tool in all architectural investigation, convenient for the analysis of architectural forms. Graphic representation can be very diverse, but in referring to a freehand drawing, rapidly executed with achromatic techniques, it appears as a schematic idea sketch that describes architectural concepts.

BRIEF DESCRIPTION OF ARCHITECTURAL CONCEPTS
Our aim is not to describe in these brief lines a whole theory of architectural composition, but it is essential to have a minimal knowledge in order to understand the concepts and, at the same time, understand many of the drawings.

Schematic idea sketch showing the project for a house with three patios by Mies van der Rohe. The whole dwelling is isolated from the exterior by a tall wall. Example of compact architecture.

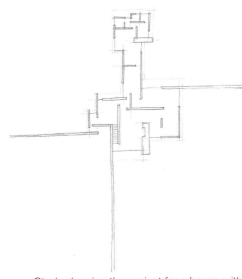

Study showing the project for a house with brick walls by Mies van der Rohe. The walls extend toward the exterior of the dwelling, opening it to the surroundings. Example of extensive architecture.

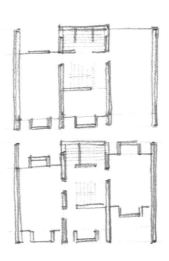

Schematic analysis showing the project for homes in Ahmadabad, India, by Louis Kahn. The supporting structure of the house is sustained on bearing walls, which allows for less flexible spaces.

Schematic idea sketch showing the project for the unbuilt Adler House (Philadelphia, Pennsylvania), by Louis Kahn. The spaces are square and are supported by robust columns that permit less rigid spaces.

Anyone who conceives an architectural work aspires to create a habitat or place of shelter and an assembly where people can go about their lives and also a place that protects them from the inclemency of the outdoors, while still integrating them into the surroundings. In order to achieve this, a program of requirements is defined and a proposal for a construction system, together with formal and organizational diagrams and financial budgets. With regard to the form, the surrounding volume of a dwelling can be compact or extensive, with a clear geometry or a grid structure; it can be the fruit of a composition of volumes, in free or organic form, or frame itself in a surrounding structure. The space will be defined by horizontal and vertical surfaces. The principal horizontal surface is the roof, held up by supporting walls or by columns. The form of the roof is bound to the vertical construction system, which might be flat or inclined, vaulted or supported by beams. The vertical surfaces limit the space laterally and, depending on their structural importance, they are more or less perforated by openings that facilitate access for the users and provide light to the interior spaces (also defined by the interior walls). The space will appear more or less fluid, open or closed, according to the communication between the interior and exterior areas. The ensemble remains connected by the floor on which we move around.

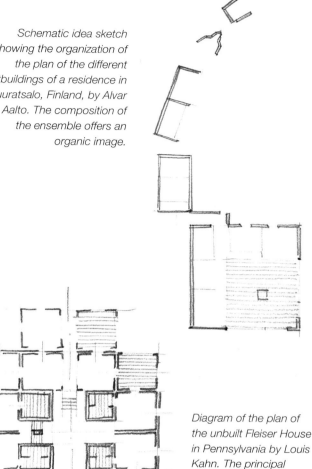

Schematic idea sketch showing the organization of the plan of the different outbuildings of a residence in Muuratsalo, Finland, by Alvar Aalto. The composition of the ensemble offers an organic image.

Diagram of the plan of the unbuilt Fleiser House in Pennsylvania by Louis Kahn. The principal criterion of the composition here is the symmetry.

Study of the plan for the R. Wright House by Frank Lloyd Wright, generated from a fusion of circular forms.

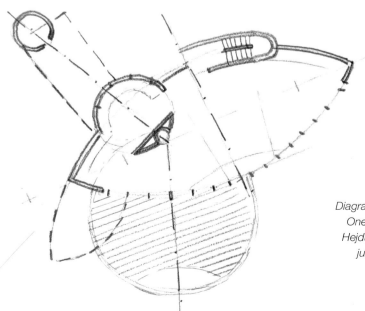

Diagram of the plan for the One-half House by John Hejduk, composed of the juxtaposition of simple geometric forms.

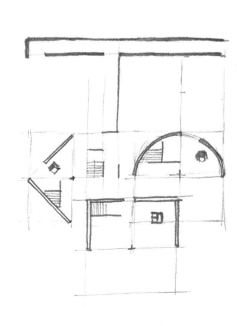

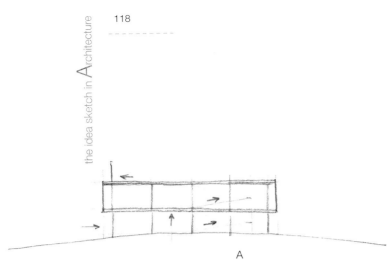

Section showing vertical circulation from the plans for the Ville Savoye, Poissy, France, by Le Corbusier.

A

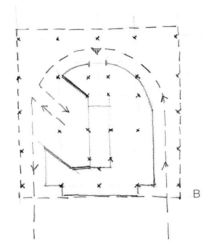

Diagram showing access for vehicles and how the ground floor accommodates their turning radius.

B

FORMAL ANALYSIS OF A PROJECT

The best way to understand these concepts is to illustrate, through idea sketches, the process of analysis of an architectural work. In this case, we have chosen a unique residence, the Ville Savoye, constructed near Poissy, France, between 1929 and 1931 by Le Corbusier. This building, a single-family residence in the middle of a field on a gentle hill with distant views in almost every direction, was ahead of its time, and in it the designer laid the foundations of modern and contemporary architecture.

In order to take full advantage of the site, the residence is divided into two levels: the ground floor, where the entrance, parking, and adjoining spaces are found, and the upper floor, where all of the living space is located (A). That division is exemplified in the circular, fluid geometric formalization, adapted for the ground floor to accommodate the turning of vehicles, and in another static, closed, compact, and prismatic formalization for the upper level (B).

The designer connects the two with a horizontal axis of symmetry where the entrance, the ramp, and the stairway are arranged in vertical communication (C).

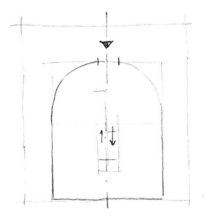

Diagram of the ground floor, where symmetry is combined with the juxtaposition of the curved and rectangular forms in the plan.

C

Analysis of circulation through the expansion of the Neues Museum, 1994–1997, in Berlin, Germany, by David Chipperfield, with the goal of incorporating the existing logic in the expansion.

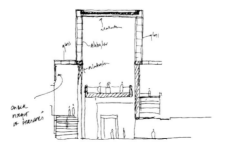

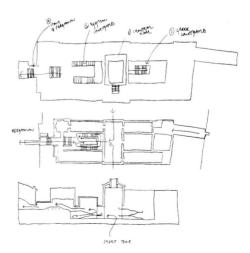

Ville Savoye by Le Corbusier.

The roofs or slabs are supported by very thin, circular concrete columns that form a network or grid, allowing for a freer distribution of the different areas whose curved walls define each space (D and E). That freedom and spatial flexibility is reproduced in the facade walls on the upper floor. They contain a succession of long, expansive windows that open the interior spaces to the surroundings while also making clear their non-structural character (F).
The geometric game, which sometimes continues and sometimes does not, orders the spaces. This is manifested on the second floor by an imaginary diagonal line that separates the public spaces (dining room, living room, and terrace) from the private ones (bedrooms) (G). The simple act of approaching the house and reaching its highest point becomes an architectural journey that allows us to penetrate the volume of the construction and ultimately leads to the roof, where a window frames the distant landscape (H).

Idea sketch in axonometric perspective for the expansion of the Prado Museum, Madrid, Spain, by Rafael Moneo, showing the relationship between the different parts of the whole structure.

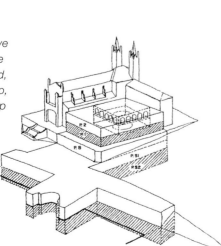

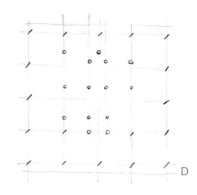

D

Diagram of the structural grid that shows how the apparent order is broken in order to adapt itself to the program.

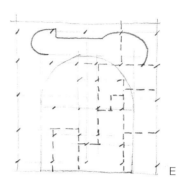

E

Diagram of the structural grid of the different floors and the interior enclosures. This diagram illustrates the formal freedom allowed by the structure of columns.

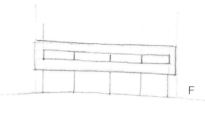

F

Diagram of one facade, which shows how the structure of columns permits very extensive windows.

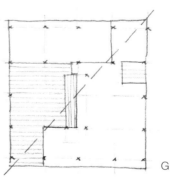

G

Diagram showing the organization of the spaces on the second floor. Here, a compound geometric criterion, its diagonal, separates the public spaces (living room, terrace) from the private ones (bedrooms and bathrooms).

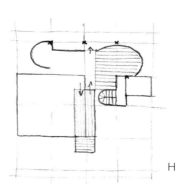

H

Diagram of the roof showing the final point of the itinerary that began on the ground floor.

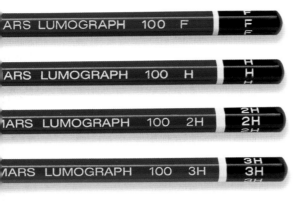

Using the

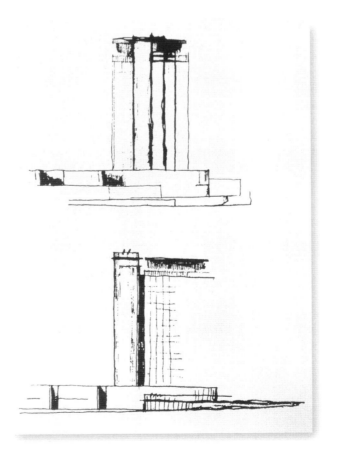

JOSEP ANTONI CODERCH
ELEVATIONS FROM THE EXPANSION OF THE ESCUELA TÉCNICA SUPERIOR DE ARQUITECTURA , BARCELONA , SPAIN , SHOWN IN RELATION TO THE EXISTING BUILDING.

idea sketch.
Analysis and simulation.
To illustrate the common practice

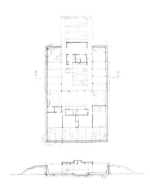

of the architectural idea sketch, we concentrate on the refinement of the concept, which is better suited to the aims of this book than the work of ideation, which pertains strictly to the professional arena.

In the refinement of the concept of a residential project, a more elaborate and academic drawing is produced so that it can be understood.

And in order to develop such a drawing, we have chosen as a model a series of residential projects (most of them unbuilt) from the American Case Study House (CSH) program. This program was developed immediately after World War II to offer the public low-cost, quality architectural models by known architects, under the auspices of *Arts and Architecture* magazine.

suggesting Volume
with shadows

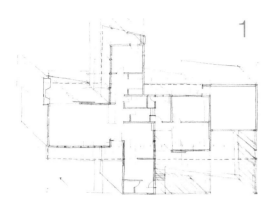

the project chosen represents an unbuilt house, the work of Richard Neutra, from the CSH program, conceived in 1945 as low-cost housing for middle-class families on the West Coast.

A large tree defined the site intended for the house. Outdoor life went on around the tree, which provided protection from the sun with the orientation of the different surroundings. The solution given, similar to other works of this period by the same designer, is based on a construction of columns and beams of wood, covered with boards or veneer of the same material. The pavement is of natural stone, which is introduced in the interior, together with the large windows, to enhance the relationship between the architecture and its surroundings.

1. On the plan, lines are used to calculate the shadows cast by the exterior enclosures where the inclination of the roof stands out.

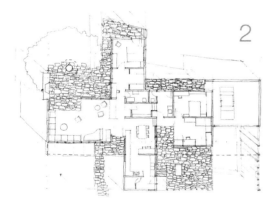

2. The texture of the stone is included to show graphically the communication between the interior and the exterior. Likewise, the interior furnishings are drawn to indicate the different uses of the rooms.

3. The shadows of the final version are drawn with linear shading that follows the direction of the light.

The shadows are always drawn after the textures, reinforcing them, if necessary, in order to avoid errors of interpretation.

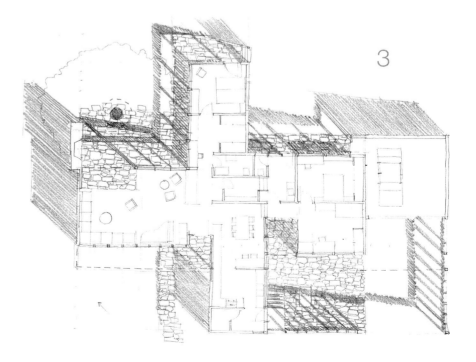

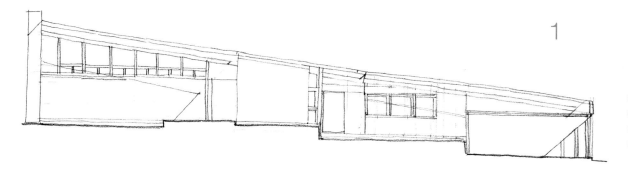

1. The shadows are calculated on an elevation, marking their outline.

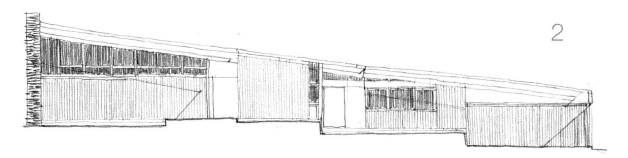

2. Next, the textures of the wood panels and glass are represented.

PLAN AND ELEVATION WITH SHADOWS

In an effort to suggest the third dimension in the representation of the plan, shadows projected by the exterior vertical enclosures of the project are used (once the roof is eliminated), and their extension is defined with a row of strokes.

The interior shadows are not drawn because the result could become unintelligible if they were superimposed on the interior distribution, particularly in some of the narrow spaces. The adopted convention is the sun located at 45° from the south (southwest), so that the direction of the shadows corresponds to the logical shadows of the project. With the inclination of 45°, the height of each element is equal to the extension of its shadow.

First, the plan is drawn, proportioned according to an approximate graphic scale that takes as reference a bed 2 m (6½ ft) long (see page 122). Then, the cast shadows are calculated using the same scale, and the furnishings as well as the texture of the natural stone pavement are added. The shadows are completed with linear shading that follows the orientation of the light on the floor.

In the selected west elevation (on this page), the same strategy is applied, but here the graphic scale is defined by the door, which also extends about 2 m (6½ ft) in height. The shadows are cast against the roof and its eaves.

3. The final version, with the shadows filled in, takes into account the different materials, with emphasis on the materials of darker tone.

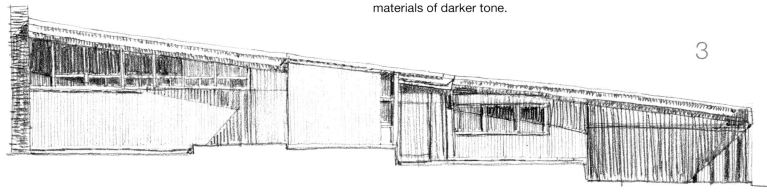

Views
of the ensemble

If one has to describe a group of houses that collectively present an interesting and clear arrangement, the best approach is a representation from an elevated point of view. The idea sketch can be either an axonometric view or a perspective view, but the first is preferable because distances and relative sizes can be drawn with greater agility and rigor.

ENSEMBLE OF THREE RESIDENCES

We will consider a collection of homes built as part of the CSH program, numbers 23A, 23B, and 23C, in La Jolla, California, in 1959–1960, the work of Killingsworth, Brady & Smith.

The group consists of three buildings with flat roofs and cubic volume, supported by very thin metal columns and very light partitions of glass and wood panels.
All three are organized on two different levels along one general axis and one individual axis and these, without becoming symmetrical, make each building appear ordered and show that the ensemble possesses clear axiality.

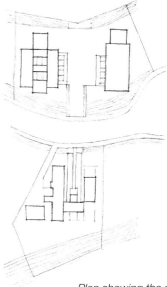

Plan showing the roof of the ensemble that we are studying.

We begin with the freehand drawing in a plan projection of the whole, once oriented. The graphic scale is approximate, each home measured according to the grid of the pavement, which we estimate at 1 m (3 ft).

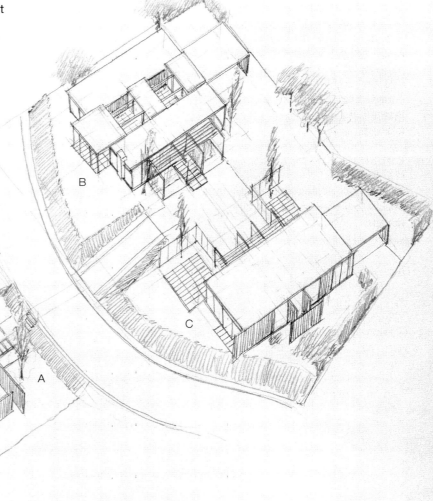

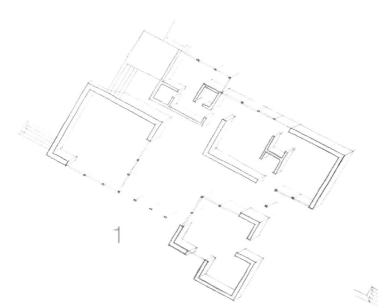

1

1. The contours of the shadows are calculated on the plan with an angle of inclination from the sun and the desired orientation of the plan.

The direction of the shadows and the orientation of the floor must be calculated beforehand to avoid everything ending up in shadow.

2

2. Then, the heights of the plan projection are arranged on the plan, toward the bottom, to avoid concealing part of the floor, and the contours are moved to the new position.

3

The general axis is reinforced by a very ceremonial entrance to house A framed by a long pool, a motif that is repeated in the entrances of the other two homes, creating a physical barrier and, in combination with some pergolas, providing climatic comfort. The large floor-to-ceiling picture windows extend the interior outward. Since house A lies one floor below houses B and C, its roof level serves as a reference for the ground floors of the other two. To complete the rough design, the vertical surfaces are drawn with rectilinear striping in their planes, and the surroundings are indicated.

VOLUMETRIC ANALYSIS
OF A PLAN

For this analysis we have chosen another unbuilt low-cost house from the CSH program, number 5, the work of Whitney R. Smith. This residence was designed for any building site. It is characterized by a variety of enclosed areas, set apart from one other by bearing walls. The roof is flat, forming an intermediate space or loggia that is open to the outdoors, where daily life unfolds.

The process for this axonometric is the same, with the addition of the cast shadows and the shades of the interior and exterior walls. These shadows make the drawing more expressive and join the different settings that define the whole.

3. Finally, shading with linear strokes is added, eliminating any unnecessary lines in order to avoid confusion.

any building settles into the site on which its foundation lies, integrating itself more or less depending on the level where domestic activity unfolds. These relationships are evident in the section of the site and the building.

Project, site and placement

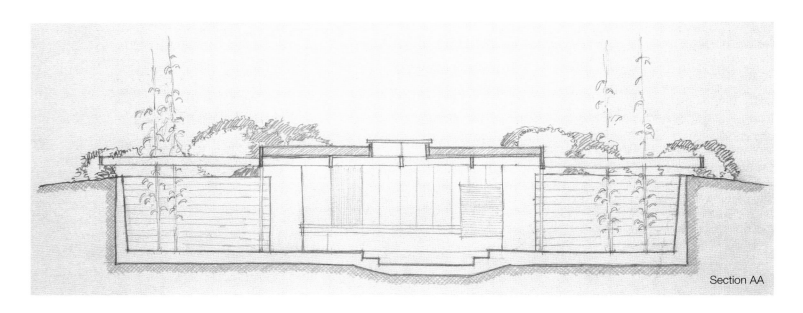

Section AA

Once we have studied the plan, starting with its drawing, we draw the section type. We add atmosphere with a variety of vegetation represented schematically, and we draw the adjacent terrain.

Diagram of the general plan and a selected section of the residence.

Plan

Section AA

EARTH-SHELTERED BUILDING

The most typical example is a building situated on a slope, as in the Guardiola House shown in chapter 1 (page 14). But the residence that is virtually buried in the ground represents a unique case. Here, the space is closed to the exterior, protected from views and from the surroundings, and open to interior patios.

An interesting example is the unbuilt project, CSH number 24, 1961, work of A. Quincy Jones. The intent in this case was to create a collection of more than 100 houses that would be partially buried, forming an undulating terrain of artificial dunes covered with grass from which the flat roofs would project, with pergolas to cover the interior patios.

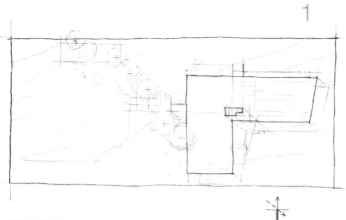

1

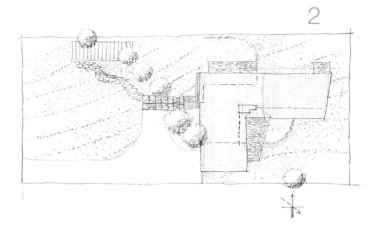

2

PLACEMENT OF A HOUSE ON A SITE

The chosen example is CSH number 13, an unbuilt residential project for a site near Los Angeles, designed for the program in 1946 by Richard Neutra.

As in the previously discussed house by Neutra, cast shadows have been employed again, but now with the roof included. In this way, an aerial view of the building shows where the shadows connect the structure to the terrain, and any irregularities.

To further clarify the design, the shadows of the trees, which the architect considered important to keep in his project, are calculated. Had it been built, the house would have been integrated with its surroundings from the start. The shadows have been drawn along a logical orientation, given the location of the project, but simplified to 45° (northwest), with an inclination also of 45°.

Thus, once the plan is set in a layout and a graphic scale of reference is chosen, the cast shadows correspond to the height of the different surfaces. To give life to the drawing, the texture of the stone of the terraces and pavements, the metal roof, as well as the trees and grass of the garden, are represented.

1. We begin by creating a layout of the site, with fine contour lines, that shows the position of the trees, the top floor of the residence, and the outline of the shadows.

2. Then the texture of the pavement and the roof is added and the trees are given volume.

3. We finish by drawing the shadows in the direction of the light and reinforcing them at those points where the texture might be confusing.

3

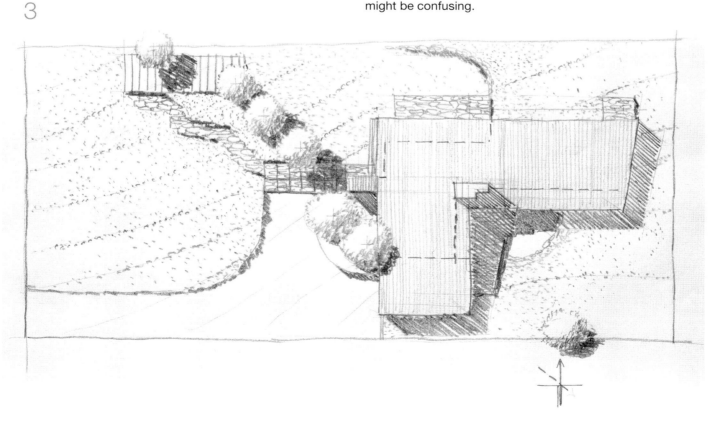

relationship of Spaces on different levels

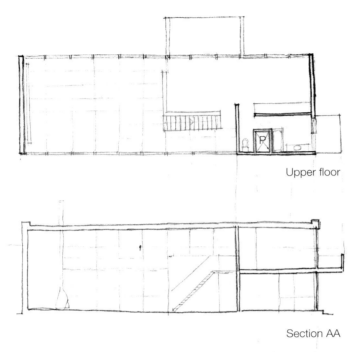

Upper floor

Section AA

When the plans for a residence involve various levels, one of the possibilities for integrating them is to make the upper spaces open onto the lower level, establishing a visual relationship between them. This communication is portrayed graphically in sections, which capture the common vertical space.

The example chosen is the section perspective for an unbuilt project by Don Knorr for the program, CHS number 19. The example illustrates how this representation allows us to visualize the appearance of the resulting space. The residence consists of three cubic spaces, starting with a modular structure of very light metal and wood partitions, sheet metal, and lots of wood. One space contains the children's bedrooms and guest bedrooms, and another holds the garage, both on the ground floor. The third and main space houses the kitchen and a sitting room and, above, the parents' study-bedroom, which overlooks the living room with double-height ceiling.

The resulting ensemble opens laterally onto the adjacent outdoor spaces by means of extensive picture windows. Covered passages connect the different structures.

Section of upper floor and ground floor with diagram of the chosen frontal perspective.

1. The section, in which the ventilation patio P has been removed for simplification, shows the different partitions as receding. The steps in the staircase are represented in the plan and the elevation. They are then transferred to the inclined plane by applying Thales' theorem.

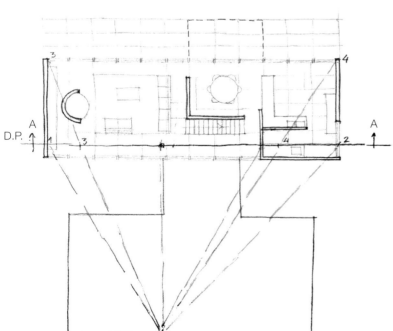

Ground floor

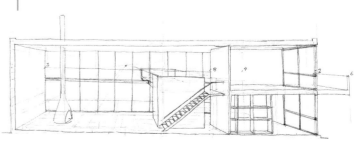

PERSPECTIVE SECTION

To draw the perspective section, a plan is marked with a grid to graphic scale. The position of the observer is determined and the drawing plane is positioned to coincide with the plane of the section, in which the different heights are seen in their true size.

The observer is located high up, in the middle of the double-height space. This position would be impossible for a real observer, but it provides the opportunity to capture all the spaces from a single point of view.

The points that define the edges of the rear wall are extended, and we transfer them to the section drawn on another sheet of paper. In the process, the perpendicular edges of the project are extended with respect to the observer at the center of vision or vanishing point. This procedure is repeated for each of the rear planes of the different rooms shown in the section.

The Thales theorem is applied to the wall of the library in order to divide the flooring in perspective.

The strategy practiced here is valid for other types of representation—for example, for the drawing of a wall in a sketch, or to give texture to a partition in an idea sketch, or for shading in a thumbnail sketch.
If one is not very sure, it is always best to try the approach first.

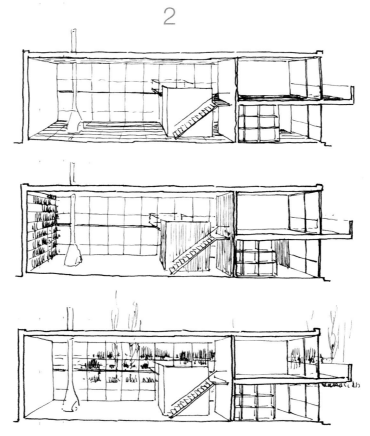

2

2. To reinforce the sensation of depth, we suggest sketching the representation on tracing paper, first with the flooring, then with the texture of the wooden partitions, and finally with the texture of the landscape in the background.

3. Using a mix of the three previous sketches, the last step is to complete the initial layout by bringing it to life with furnishings and a human figure

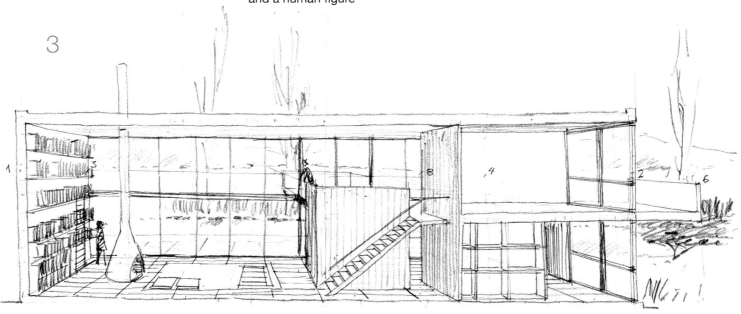

3

Frontal views of the space

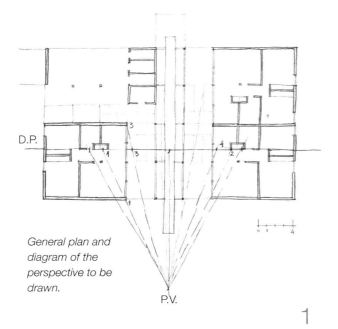

General plan and diagram of the perspective to be drawn.

D.P.

P.V.

1

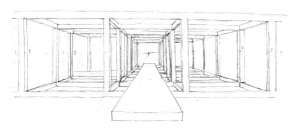

from the CSH program we have chosen the built project CSA number 1 in Phoenix, Arizona, designed by A. Beadle and A. Dailey in 1963. It is an ensemble of three small apartments developed from a three-dimensional metal structure on the ground floor.

FRONTAL VIEW OF A SYMMETRICAL SPACE

The entrances are very symmetrical, deep settings in which the prevailing order of the columns and girders or beams forms a narrow space.

A frontal perspective reinforces the depth of the represented setting, and when this setting is symmetrical, it becomes even more so in a frontal view, situating us right at the very center—the place chosen for this idea sketch. The point of view and the drawing plane are arranged over the floor plane to coincide with a corner or clear edge, and over this the farthest columns of the main facade are projected in order to define the field of vision.

The horizon line is transferred to another sheet of paper as in the previous example, and the process is completed.

1. It is advisable to begin the layout of the idea sketch with the foreground so that closest columns and beams gradually conceal the most distant ones, which will barely need to be suggested.

2. The drawing is finished by emphasizing the texture of the pavement.

2

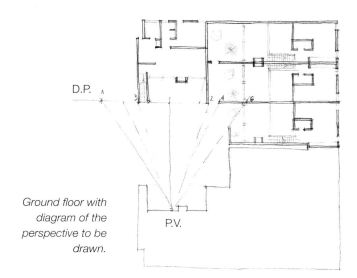

D.P.

P.V.

Ground floor with diagram of the perspective to be drawn.

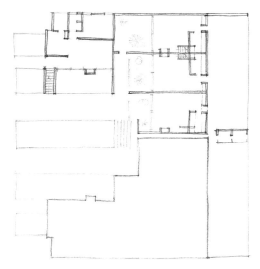

Upper floor necessary to complete the work.

ASYMMETRIC FRONTAL VIEW AND REFLECTIONS ON A POOL

The second example represented is CSA number 2, an unbuilt project designed by Killingsworth and Brady in 1964. The project is composed of 10 small residences developed on two levels and symmetrically arranged around a central pond.

The process is the same as before, but based on a frontal asymmetric view from the side of the ensemble, with the goal of studying the reflections on the pool.

The reflections are obtained by vertically extending the different edges downward using the same dimensions, but arranged in the opposite direction and measured from their base. In this way, the edges that cross over the pool define the reflection. Then the process is repeated with the horizontal edges.

To enhance the impression of reflection, the line of the projected edges is blurred, and at the same time, the pool is given life by adding aquatic plants and a light texture of lines that represent the water.

1

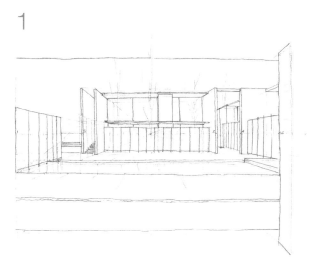

2

1. First, the proposed one-point perspective is laid out with lines.

2. We finish by blocking in the pavement of the central area and schematically drawing only the trees in the background.

Visual analysis
of an interior environment

The proposed subject is project number 26 by Killingsworth, Brady and Smith, from 1962. It is a large single-family residence with a single entrance that is almost entirely surrounded by a shallow pool.

EYE-LEVEL LINEAR PERSPECTIVE
The repetitive vertical nature of the slender columns is very distinctive in this design and conveys a monumental and rhythmic atmosphere in which the extensive entrance porch, the ample living room, and interior patio stand out.
The chosen view is from a position next to the living room chimney (C), looking toward the entrance porch through the perimeter picture windows.

The observer is located on the plan and the drawing plane coincides with one of the columns of the vestibule. In order to determine the vanishing points, two perpendicular lines are drawn, from the position of the observer, parallel to the grid of the plan, and extended until they cross the drawing plane.

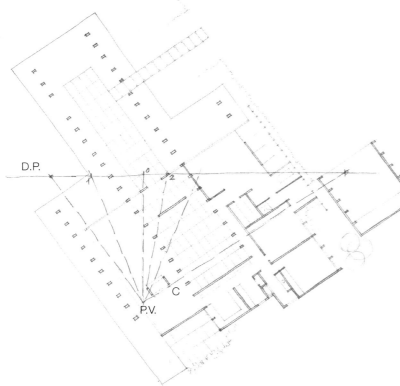

D.P.

C

P.V.

1. Initial layout of the oblique (two-point) perspective. As always, the principal edges are referenced with numbers.

2. In order to enhance the sense of depth and illustrate the appearance of the columns, the texture of the concrete bricks is drawn.

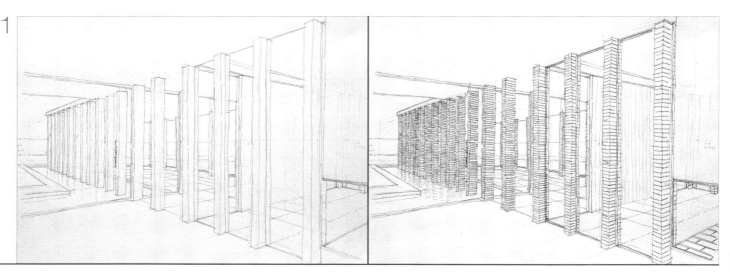

1

2

Starting with the drawing of the plan, with the aid of a small graphic scale based on the size of one of the pieces of the flooring (1 m/3 ft), the plan diagram perspective is measured and then transferred to another sheet of paper. Here, the outer edges are arranged, drawing between them as many subdivisions as there are units measured on the plan. The approximate distance at which the vanishing points will be found is marked on the ends of the horizon line.

The vertical lines passing through these edges are drawn, especially the vertical line coincident with the drawing plane. Using the new graphic scale, the height of the observer (1.5 m/5 ft) and the height of the ceiling (3 m/9 3/4 ft) are marked on this line, according to the measurements taken from the documents available.

The horizontal edges of the model are drawn and on them the relative position of all the necessary intermediate vertical edges, converging their position at ground level until they coincide with the projected vertical projection.

Once most of the columns have been represented in the foreground, the columns farthest away are added. Then, the position of the intermediate columns is determined, beginning with the columns in the foreground, by applying the Thales theorem. It is important to maintain the relative size between the two visible sides of each column throughout the perspective.

When representing the texture of the concrete bricks, their horizontal joint is drawn in all of the columns so that as they accumulate in the distance, they darken the drawing and reinforce the depth of the perspective.

To create the receding texture of the concrete blocks that form the columns, it is helpful to draw, with the help of a sheet of paper as a sort of ruler, the joints located every 5 or 10 blocks so that they serve as a guide for drawing the remaining joints.

3

3. The reflection on the pool is resolved in the same way as in the previous example. To suggest the use of the different setting, some furnishings are represented schematically. Finally, the drawing is finished with the addition of some ornamental plants and the texture of the closest pavement.

view of an Interior-
exterior space

We have chosen an unbuilt project for a greenhouse-residence, CSH number 4, work of Ralph Rapson, from 1945. It is a prototype for an ecological dwelling from that period.

OBLIQUE PERSPECTIVE
WITH SHADOWS AND ATMOSPHERE

The residence consists of two parallel bodies of metal construction with partitions of wood panels and wired glass. Cutting across them is an interior garden covered by a pergola. The planting in the interior garden, in the form of parterres, serves both as a vestibule and as a play area, extending along the interior of the residence. A system of hot- and cold-water pipes would cover the whole pavement for climate control.

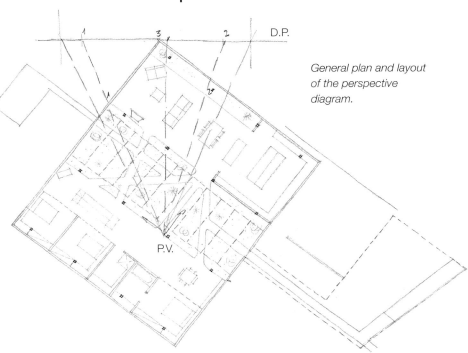

General plan and layout of the perspective diagram.

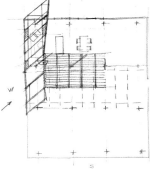

Calculation on the plan of the shadows in the area of the chosen view.

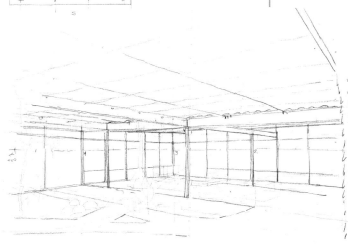

1

The highlight of this project is the gardened interior space, which receives direct natural light from outside, and the shaded interior settings overlooking the decorative and vegetable gardens, which afford a view of the desert landscape beyond.

On the roughly measured diagram of the plan, taking as base measurement one of the planting beds, a point of view is chosen for the oblique perspective so that the garden with its pathways appears in the foreground. The shaded living room lies at middle distance, and in the background, the exterior landscape.

The drawing plane is located on the farthest exterior edge (numbered 3 in the diagram above) and two more edges are projected, one to each side of the principal point, to define the scenic box and the extremes of the angle of vision with its respective vanishing points.

1. Initial linear layout of the view.

2

3

2. The elements of the scene are progressively incorporated.

3. The planting, primarily cactus and vegetables, gives atmosphere to the space. The furnishings are added lightly, with a pair of shrubs to frame the view. The wood panels, the interior pavement, and the wire latticework of the pergola are also shaded in at this point.

Next, this is transferred to another sheet where the perspective is drawn to occupy the maximum space for clear representation of the landscape in the background. The observer is positioned at a height of 1.5 m (5 ft) and the height of the roof with its varied angles in the different areas of the residence is determined.

Measurements are calculated on the plan for the interior shadows that the roof, the central pergola, and the lateral partitions cast onto the greenhouse and the living room. The sun, situated to the southwest of the residence at an inclination of 45°, is used as a reference. At this angle, the sun produces shadows on the ground that are the same size as the height of the element in a one-point perspective.

4

4. To reinforce the pictorial nature of the scene once the shadows have been drawn, the lines that define the roof and the different elements of the landscape and the living room are further intensified, silhouetting them against the light in the background and bringing the garden closer.

the selected project is for an unbuilt residence, CSH number 6, 1945, by Richard Neutra, envisioned for a plot of land located in Omega, California. An enormous eucalyptus tree dominates the scene, lying to the northeast and occupying one of the four spaces created by the cross-shaped footprint of the residence. In the summer, most outdoor activity takes place under the shade of the tree.

Visual simulation
of a building

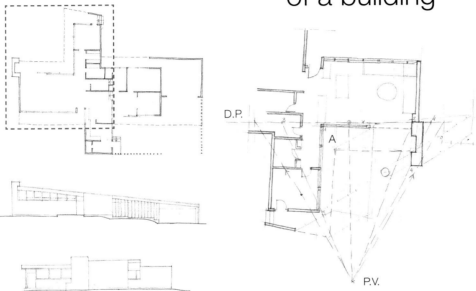

Plan and elevations necessary for creating the proposed subject. On it, the selected portion is framed, enlarged, and turned 180°.

On a portion of the rotated plan, the observer is positioned (P.V.) and the perspective and the shadows are planned.

IDEA SKETCH FOR PRESENTATION

This residence was designed in wood with an enormous inclined roof that protects the exterior spaces, on which it throws extensive shadows. The designer's use of materials such as stone and wood is notable. The simulation of these materials, the environment beneath the great eucalyptus tree, and the interior furnishings, which are visible through the immense window of the living room, is a very appropriate exercise for the culmination of this chapter.

As always, drawing begins with a diagram of the plan. The point of view is then incorporated into the plan, and the drawing plane is arranged to coincide with one corner of the patio (A), resulting in an oblique but almost frontal perspective. Thus, one of the vanishing points lies within the sheet of paper, but the other is very far away, which means that the drawing of the lines that converge on it becomes totally intuitive, without visual reference.

1. Initial layout of the view. The beams, being inclined, vanish to a point below the horizon line located on the same vertical as the normal vanishing point.

2. It is important to represent the texture of the stone; the designer used this feature to integrate the exterior and interior spaces.

1

2

The finishing touches of the idea sketch require a clean motion. It is helpful to put a fresh sheet of paper under your hand so that its movement does not smear what has already been drawn.

3

3. Now the space is given atmosphere by adding the living room furniture and the texture of the wood partitions, the interior-exterior pavement, the stone chimney, and the trunk of the eucalyptus.

Two more edges are then projected and the extremes of the angle of vision are roughly measured with an intuitive graphic scale derived from the model itself. The diagram is transferred to another sheet and adjusted to the new dimensions, defining the heights of the observer and the roof.

The shadows are calculated on the plan and then transferred to the perspective with the help of a reference grid. The cast shadows on the walls and the areas that will be seen backlit and in shade are roughly drawn.

4

4. The rough design is finished by drawing the shadows, which are reinforced in the interior areas.

the Thumbnail sketch

"TO DRAW IS, PRIMARILY, TO LOOK WITH THE EYES, TO OBSERVE, TO DISCOVER. TO DRAW IS TO LEARN TO SEE THINGS BE BORN, GROW, DEVELOP, DIE. WE MUST DRAW IN ORDER TO INTERNALIZE WHAT WE HAVE SEEN, AND THUS IT WILL REMAIN WRITTEN IN OUR MEMORY FOR THE REST OF OUR LIFE."
Le Corbusier.

intuition and intention in architectural drawing

the Thumbnail
the drawing of

sketch
architectural
Intentions.

We define the thumbnail sketch

as a freehand drawing, usually in perspective, whose principal objective is to stress one or various essential aspects of an architectural motif, regardless of the others. It is also a drawing in which intuition is valued more than precision.

For someone unfamiliar with the architectural world, the thumbnail sketch may seem like simple or imprecise representations. The expert, however, finds them very suggestive. The more powerful the underlying architectural idea expressed in a final drawing, the more abstract that drawing might be, especially if the person who creates it is also the author of the work. We think that the fastest and simplest thumbnail sketches are the most authentic examples, but reaching that level requires much practice and experience.

the Drawing and expression
of architectural concepts

beginning with the concept that defines the final drawing, clearly the stroke, the gestures, and the strategies that must be used in this representation are the freest. Prior training and experience are, therefore, a necessity, and for this reason the thumbnail sketch appears here as the final stage of the representations. Architectural ideas must take priority in the drawing, and so it is helpful to explain or, at least, clearly articulate some inherent aspects of the form and organization of the architectural space in order to better understand the thumbnail sketches that we will develop. What is described below is not intended in any way to present a theory of architecture, but rather only a systematic and objective approximation of the most characteristic features of architecture, expressed with words understandable by any reader.

Thumbnail sketch in colored pencil by Carlos Conesa showing the Palace of Dance, Valencia, Spain, by Santiago Calatrava.

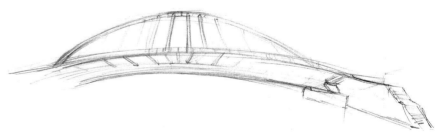

Thumbnail sketch in graphite pencil showing a pier in Rotterdam, the Netherlands, work of Bolles & Wilson.

Thumbnail sketches in graphite pencil by Carlos Conesa showing the Alameda Bridge, Valencia, Spain, by Santiago Calatrava.

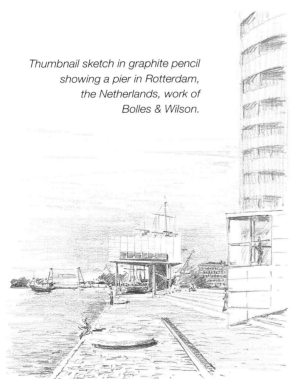

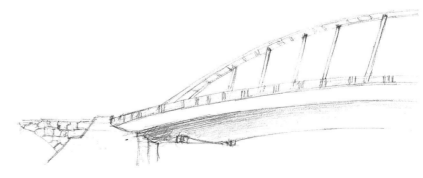

INTERIOR SPACE.
ELEMENTARY ARCHITECTURAL CONCEPTS

When we are faced with the problem of describing an architectural form in a final drawing, the most common approach is to focus on its visual values more than on its internal structure or other geometric parameters that would require further specialized training in architecture.

We will look, therefore, at perceptual values such as whether a space or architectural form presents clear symmetry; whether it is orthogonal or organic; whether it has a physical connection with the exterior or is self-contained; whether it is an isolated element or forms part of an ensemble. Or, within a building, whether the relationship between the different spaces is clear or not, whether they are straight, tall, low, etc.; whether they form a sequence and invite visitors, as in the case of a hallway, or they are static, like a large circular living room. We will observe how the limits are defined, the walls, roofs, and floors, with the assumption that any space has at least a floor on which to move, some walls, and usually a roof, which can present different forms, from flat to vaulted; whether very obvious elements exist in the structure, like columns and beams, through which, furthermore, light may penetrate the interior. We must understand how the space is lit, how the walls look, whether the texture of the materials is smooth or wrinkled, their appearance, and so on.

It is very important to review the whole setting and to carefully select a frame for the view that best describes the most characteristic aspect of the architecture in a single drawing.

Thumbnail sketch in pencil showing the Kenneth Laurent House in Illinois by Frank Lloyd Wright.

We have taken as a model the National Library in Paris by Dominique Perrault. First, with arms extended, the writing pad (drawing plane D.P.) is positioned in front of the model, concealing it.

The horizon line (H.L.) is then drawn, and, using the edge of the sketchpad, the vanishing points (V.P.1 and V.P.2) are added to the horizon line, following the lines of the cornices.

V.P.1   H.L.   V.P.2

The pad is moved downward until the corners of the towers (A, B, C, D) appear above it, and we mark them on the paper.

A B   C   D

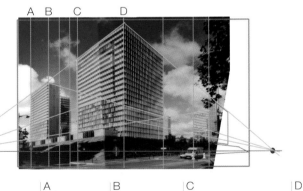

In the same way, the ends 1 and 2 of vertical edge closest to us (D) are obtained.
Then the pad is moved to one side, following line H.L., and the process is repeated with few more edges. On this base, we draw the rest of the scene approximately. This is the final drawing resulting from the process described.

EXTERIOR SPACE.
FUNDAMENTAL CONCEPTS

In the definition of an exterior space, which is to say, of the immediate exterior surroundings of the architectural structure, those elements closest to the structure have special importance—elements like the vegetation, the pavement and its texture, the different contours, the fences or peripheral walls and facades that surround it, as well as the distant or more distant landscape that completes the scenery. We must consider the scale of the landscape with respect to the observer, which confers very different perceptual qualities. It is not the same to be on a tree-lined path as in a meadow or a forest. Obviously, the sensation perceived in a Spanish patio is not at all like the experience of contemplating a Japanese garden.

The first element to be considered is the point of view, since this denotes the accessibility of the space, the naturalness of the place from the person observing toward the point where the spectator's attention is focused. Secondly, the layout and the composition of the thumbnail sketch are very important, since once again the principal motif must be considered, using its planes and elements of composition to lead the gaze of the observer toward the central theme. The entourage

|A |B |C |D

to V.P.1

1D

to V.P.2

2D

Thumbnail sketch in graphite pencil showing the terrace of the Ville Savoye, Poissy, France, by Le Corbusier.

Thumbnail sketch in graphite pencil showing the Stahl House, West Hollywood, California, by Pierre Koening.

(people, furnishings, etc.) should receive very light treatment, primarily to indicate the human scale of the place, since the surroundings would be better reflected in a photograph, which is not the theme of this book. Leaving the anecdotes aside, the architectural values should be the focus.

The pavement is usually another key element because it defines the utilization of the space and establishes the continuities and barriers. Therefore, the treatment of the textures and of the materials that fashion the pavement represents a basic tool for explaining the details in its design. Other basic elements include the vegetation, trees and shrubs whose detail will vary with distance, as well as the background landscape, which helps to reinforce the sensation of depth that the final drawing ought to evoke. Each basic idea must be reflected in a single final drawing, and every aspect— stroke, texture, shading, and composition— should reinforce the architectural intentionality of the drawing.

Thumbnail sketch in black pencil of Korsula, Croatia.

Thumbnail sketch in black pencil of Sant Marti Vell, Girona, Spain.

THE URBAN LANDSCAPE AND ITS COMPONENTS

All the strategies explained for drawing an exterior space also apply for the thumbnail sketch of an urban setting, which should highlight the qualities that make the scene attractive from an architectural point of view. These include the proportions of the setting, the articulation of its enclosures, its transparency, its human scale—attributes of its urban architecture and design. One important aspect is the silhouette of the buildings that define it. The upper limit of their facades, where they meet the sky, constitutes a border that always draws the attention of the viewer.

The shading with juxtaposed lines is fundamental in the composition of the thumbnail sketch. Here the vegetation should have the same consideration as a wall or fence and, according to its importance and structure, receive the appropriate treatment.

In the perception of the urban landscape, the settings that define the image of a city are of special importance. Although this is usually very subjective, it can be clarified if we stop to think about memories and real life experiences and their characteristic images. A good guide for tackling these scenes would be to draw the common routes or paths, the visual limits or linear elements that are not crossed and that define boundaries, like the bank of a river or the shoreline; the neighborhoods of the mid-sized city with very characteristic settings that define that city and make it recognizable; steeples, town squares, or gathering places; the points of historical reference of any city, such as monuments, statues; and what defines its skyline or a distant image of the skyline.

It is not always feasible to make the thumbnail sketch from an optimal location in which the sun illuminates the scene. One has to adapt in each case, sometimes resigning oneself to focusing on the silhouette or the volume of the ensemble.

Thumbnail sketch in black pencil of Saint Gilles, France.

FROM THE CONCEPT TO THE DRAWING

Once these concepts have been clarified, once the observer has learned to look, they must be committed to memory and kept in mind during the execution of the thumbnail sketch. Given that this is the culminating point in a whole process of graphic apprenticeship, it helps to stop and review certain concepts, applying knowledge about systems of representation, types of perspective, etc. Will the perspective be centered or oblique? Will we draw it with a silhouette or lines or shading? Is the setting characterized by shadows or by its details and textures? Will we use graphite or ink, depending on the extent and density of the shading? The resulting drawing should be a synthesis of everything described. We will produce a whole, the most expressive representation, loaded with intentions, economical in time and in resources, and the most suggestive of the place. That is the thumbnail sketch, at least from our point of view.

Thumbnail sketch with fountain pen of Cartagena, Colombia, by Álvaro Siza.

thumbnail Sketches
for travel

thumbnail sketches executed during a trip constitute an exceptional case. These arise when someone interested in architecture wishes to recreate a scene, and in order to learn the scene and understand it, the best approach is to draw rather than photograph it. Drawing obliges us to choose what we want to emphasize from the scene and to discard the superfluous or picturesque. Although at first sight, the view might seem very photographic, that quality is irrelevant from an architectural point of view.

In order to distinguish between what interests and what does not, a greater knowledge of the architectural structure is required as well as a commitment to study the place more slowly, while drawing. Thus the characteristics are determined, always choosing an architectural point of view; the scene becomes simplified, and, ultimately, one learns to see and choose in order to represent it rapidly on paper.

Thumbnail sketch in black pencil from a trip to Sant Marti d'Empúries, Girona, Spain.

Thumbnail sketches in graphite pencil from a trip to Munich, Germany.

Thumbnail sketches, in collections or travel notebooks, were once a traditional method of compiling architectural experiences, before the age of photography. It was common to take trips for the purpose of copying architectural models from distant places.

Nowadays, in spite of technological advances, thumbnail sketches continue to be a recommended practice and a vital and unforgettable experience in the study of architecture.

The creation of drawings, being immediate, requires a common graphic medium, one that is familiar and easy to carry, like a pencil or a felt-tipped pen, and a support, such as a hardcover notebook. Notable examples of this practice are the travel notebooks of thumbnail sketches by Le Corbusier, Alvar Aalto, Arne Jacobsen, and Louis Kahn, just to name a few modern architects worth consulting.

Thumbnail sketches from a trip to Greece, by Arne Jacobsen.

Thumbnail sketches from a trip to Marrakesh, Morocco, by Alvar Alto.

Space in

ARNE JACOBSEN.
THUMBNAIL SKETCH IN INK.

architecture.
An architectural space is the result of space

wrapping or embracing a fragment of a space with different enclosures, pavements, and roofs, and doing so in a way that the result will protect us from inclement weather and that, moreover, may be pleasant from a perceptual point of view. This is one of the premises of architecture. In order to capture that sensation, to suggest the perception of the space in the thumbnail sketch, the one-point perspective provides the best representation. This space can be the result of a formal strategy to create settings by accumulating or juxtaposing elements and forms, positive space that leads to lighter, more open architectural structures, or it can result from subtracting or sculpting a mass, creating holes or negative space that leads to denser, more confined architectural structures. Once this is captured, it should be represented in a deliberate way with a drawing composed of lines and shading, accumulated strokes and tones.

the Interior architectural space

Thumbnail sketch in graphite pencil showing the house-studio of Rudolf M. Schindler, California.

"**a**rchitecture is an imposing game, perfect and admirable, of masses that meet under the light." This sentence, from the great master architect Le Corbusier, describes an attitude and a particular way of understanding architecture based on the use of simple volumes in its conception, but also on the fact that it is light, how it accesses the interior and how we control it by means of openings, that allows us to perceive the architectural structure, the spaces within and its boundaries and its appearance.

In this journey through architectural concepts, with help from the thumbnail sketch, we have decided to begin by explaining how different architects play with light, allowing it to be introduced into spaces; how they vary the shape of the openings, locating them in different places; how they bathe the walls or flood the settings and denote their texture; how they open one space to another, and so on.

THUMBNAIL SKETCH OF THE SITTING ROOM INTERIOR IN THE KOSHINO HOUSE, WORK OF TADAO ANDO

The work of this Japanese architect is characterized by very sparing use of materials like concrete, wood, even water in pools; by very simple geometric spaces of very tight proportions; and by the use of light in a symbolic way. All this contributes to the sense of mysticism in his designs, in its simplicity and a poetic privacy.

Sitting room of the Koshino House, Ashiya, Japan, by Tadao Ando.

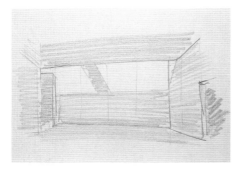

Schematic drawing of the subject in graphite pencil.

1

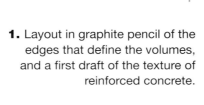

1. Layout in graphite pencil of the edges that define the volumes, and a first draft of the texture of reinforced concrete.

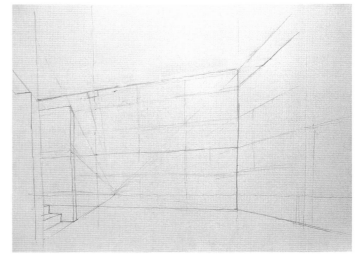

A good way to tackle a thumbnail sketch for this space relies on a technique that permits covering extensive areas easily, since we are dealing with an interior view of a relatively dark space with concrete walls whose texture requires close attention.

We will use a graphite pencil together with a graphite stick of the same hardness.

Once the point of view has been chosen, in this case from a seat on the floor since the setting is Japanese, the horizon line is drawn on the lower part of the paper, and the point of view is placed at the center. Then the vertical edges that define the space are drawn and the horizontal lines are drawn to their respective vanishing points. We use a slightly skewed one-point (technically two-point) perspective to indicate that the space is not symmetrical and that it is oriented toward one of its corners. With the graphite stick, the different surfaces are shaded according to their orientation to the light. The gradation does not have extremes because this space is lit from all sides and therefore does not exhibit great contrasts of light.

The thumbnail sketch is completed by outlining the concrete panels with the graphite pencil. Their texture is added, and at the same time the deepest areas of the shadows are shaped and darkened.

In the different stages of shading, it is helpful to protect the drawing from contact with the hand. Using a clean piece of paper is a good method.

2

2. Using a graphite stick, the shadows and surfaces are shaded with lines.

3. The pencil is also used to complete the thumbnail sketch by outlining the edges and the areas of mass.

3

THUMBNAIL SKETCH OF THE VESTIBULE INTERIOR IN STEVEN HOLL'S STRETTO HOUSE

The work of this architect is characterized by its great freedom of form. The enclosures are interrupted by free-form openings in which views of the outdoors combine with the luminous and chromatic control of the interior through the use of less severe indirect lighting. All this can be adjusted by the inhabitants. We consider the openings an interesting focus for this final drawing, shown from the inside out, with a luminous quality almost of backlighting because the interior is very dark and the exterior very bright. The many gradations produced in this narrow setting make the charcoal pencil, blended with the finger, an ideal choice. The charcoal pencil has a very broad gradation of tones, which easily display contrast, and it facilitates rapid covering of a large surface.

Vestibule of the Stretto House, Dallas, Texas, by Steven Holl.

Schematic thumbnail sketch in charcoal pencil of the architectural structure that we will study.

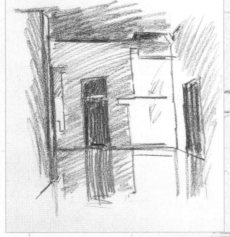

1. The setting is very lightly outlined with the charcoal pencil.

1

2

3

When blending, it is helpful to use a mask of clean paper to clearly define the shaded areas at the edges.

4

2. The process continues with shading in charcoal pencil and an initial, light blending.

3. After shading and blending, the edges are defined.

Standing in the vestibule of the residence and looking toward the entrance door, the horizon line is drawn along the middle of the paper. The point of view is located at the center, since one-point perspective seems very appropriate for this setting. The horizontal and vertical lines that define the frontal plane are lightly drawn.

Then, with the same charcoal pencil, the different surfaces are shaded with irregular strokes in a gradation: the maximum light should be the white of the illuminated exterior or its reflection on the floor, and the darkest black, that of the backlit wooden door.

This base of strokes is blended with the finger, using a piece of paper as a mask to define the borders. This process is repeated in other areas with the necessary adjustments. Finally, with a very sharp pencil or one with the edge of its lead flattened, the outlines of the woodwork on the different windows are drawn, and the shadows and details are accentuated.

4. The result of the process described.

architecture
and its surroundings

architecture is also the art of adapting the human habitat to its surroundings, and in this sense, of protecting us from the inclemency of the weather. A single program for a house can take on different forms, depending on geographic location, climate, morphology of the terrain, orientation, views, vegetation, neighboring buildings, etc. The design process moves in two different directions, reflecting two esthetic attitudes: an esthetic of contrast, when the result is a residence of rigid form, based on simple geometry, impressive or isolated from the terrain and the surroundings; and a natural esthetic, when the solution is organic, flexible, discrete, and responsive to the location. In both cases, the result should satisfy the house's occupants without visually polluting the surroundings, making scale an essential consideration. The thumbnail sketch of the context is, therefore, very helpful, both in assessing the morphology of the surroundings and in testing the result of the integration of the architectural structure in those surroundings.

Thumbnail sketch in ink of a restaurant, Leça da Palmeira, Portugal, by Alvaro Siza.

FOLIE, BY BERNARD TSCHUMI, IN LA VILLETTE PARK

This work, an architectural folly in Parc de La Villette in Paris, is a small building that is one of many buildings strewn throughout the park according to a grid. Its structure is a variant of a pattern that stems from an orthogonal metal structure in red to which modifications and additions are made and whose use ranges from a small dwelling or bar to the symbol for the entrance to the existing buildings.

Folie, *by Bernard Tschumi, Parc de La Villette, Paris, France.*

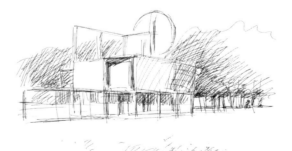

Schematic thumbnail sketch in ink of the subject of this step-by-step.

1

1. Because the technique employed here is indelible, we begin the layout with very fine lines.

2

This technique, using fine ink lines, requires patient work in order to define the masses and shadows accurately.

The result contrasts agreeably with the planted surroundings, composed of large grassy meadows with rows of slender trees. The effect of this contrast, building/surroundings, is always produced in a particular setting. In other words, every building defines its specific surroundings to human scale. In each case, this repetition in different areas of the park provides a reference for location.

In the thumbnail sketch shown here, the main intent has been to accurately represent the metallic structure with its turnbuckles, plates, etc., as well as the vegetation that surrounds it. A fountain pen was used because it is sufficiently precise to produce fine lines while providing enough contrast to suggest the texture of the grass and trees, as well as tone of the dark shadows.

The successive lines provide the layout first, then the definition of the masses and shadows with shading, and finally suggest the texture of the vegetation.

2. Little by little the juxtaposed strokes succeed in defining volumes and masses.

3. The proposed architectural structure ultimately looks like this in its surroundings.

3

the Urban space

the city is the meeting place par excellence for human beings. Over the course of history, a city is gradually shaped by a series of characteristic elements that define its image. Beginning with a point of exchange, an intersection to which temples, palaces, public buildings, and the houses or shops of the inhabitants are added along the streets and squares, the city is defined. The urban web assumes multiple configurations depending on how it is integrated into the environment. We have chosen an example in a specific geographic setting, the Netherlands, because in recent years this country has become one of the most important urban laboratories in history and a place where prestigious architects plan very interesting projects.

Thumbnail sketch in graphite pencil showing a square in Hengelo, the Netherlands, work of Bolles & Wilson.

Houses on the canal in Borneo-Sporenburg, Amsterdam, the Netherlands, by MVRDV.

Schematic thumbnail sketch of the houses in graphite pencil.

HOUSE IN BORNEO-SPORENBURG, AMSTERDAM, BY THE MVRDV FIRM

This team of architects proposes a minimal residence, very narrow and deep, following the proportions of a narrow lot, typical of the country, with the facade facing one of its famous canals. The project sits amidst others of similar character and of recent construction. It is distinguished by incorporating several floors and by managing to introduce natural light throughout the interior.

1

1. Initial layout in graphite pencil using lines that are almost orthogonal, due to the chosen point of view. The position of the hand in this phase contributes to the correct representation of the layout.

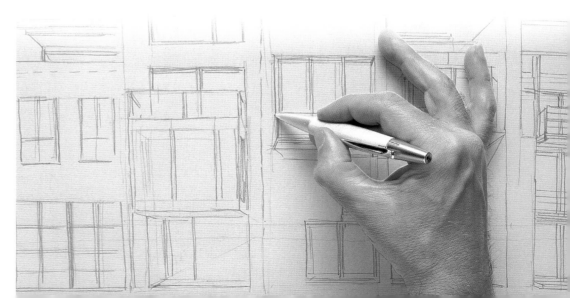

The project with its surroundings is described in a view from the other side of the canal, in keeping with the characteristic image of the city. The thumbnail sketch offers a one-point perspective, executed with graphite pencil and stick, in order to generate aptly the details of the woodwork, the shading of the shadows, and the tone of the different materials.

First, the horizon line is set in pencil at the height of an observer located at the level of the other side of the canal. Then the divisions of the different lots are determined, as well as the levels or floors of each one; these lines are extended over the water in order to define the reflections that are always in the vertical of the lines that initiate them. Next, the deepest parts are shaded with the graphite stick: the water of the canal, the sky, and the tone of the materials. Finally, the details of the woodwork are defined and the cast shadows are emphasized with the graphite pencil, and the reflections are made lighter and more blurred with the graphite stick.

2

2. Shading is begun with the graphite stick.

3. The final result is attained with outlining in pencil.

3

Isolated residence in a square in the Hague, the Netherlands, by Alvaro Siza.

Schematic thumbnail sketch in graphite pencil of the proposed exercise.

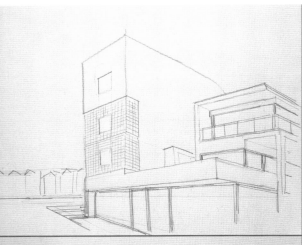

1

1. The edges that define the volumes are considered when sketching the layout with a graphite pencil.

2. With the graphite stick, the texture of the brick as well as the pavement and the dark areas are enhanced according to their distance and orientation.

RESIDENCE IN DER VENNE PARK
BY ALVARO SIZA

In a newly created square in the Hague, this residence stands as a building-monument. The project is characteristic of the designer's way of working. He proposes on the one hand a simple but highly articulated form, integrated into its surroundings with the use of brick, typical of Dutch architecture; on the other hand, its size or scale as a single building is isolated in a setting of attached residences; and, finally, the special shape of the volume possesses a flat main facade and curving rear facades so that the space flows around it. The result can be produced in a final drawing with oblique perspective from the point of view of someone seated on a bench in the square at several yards distance so that the building can be seen at the same time as the facades that surround the square. A graphite stick is used, as well as a graphite pencil with the point flattened in order to reproduce the brick walls. The layout and the tonal values are the same as in other final drawings in graphite.

2

3. In order to complete the thumbnail sketch, it is given definition with the graphite pencil, and the surroundings are added.

3

SUBSIDIZED HOUSING BY ALVARO SIZA IN SCHILDERSWIJK WARD

The third thumbnail sketch example is of a street in the same area of the Hague, also the work of Alvaro Siza. An equivalent technique is used and a similar, though less oblique, layout. The street itself is of interest: its width, the height of the neighboring buildings, and its setting, as well as the facade of the residences, which overlook a square. This unique point is characteristic of this type of neighborhood and the reason for our interest.

The setting repeats the same constants as the previous thumbnail sketch, but on a sunny day with scattered clouds; the sky is represented more expressively and the projected shadows with greater intensity.

Subsidized housing in the Hague, the Netherlands, by Alvaro Siza.

The sensation of depth can be achieved with density of lines, using care and always observing the vanishing points.

1

Schematic thumbnail sketch in graphite pencil of the architectural proposal.

1. The edges that define the volumes are laid out with penciled lines.

2

2. Then the negative spaces and contours are outlined and better defined, and the pavement and the vegetation are suggested.

3. The setting and the definition of the ensemble complete this thumbnail sketch.

3

architecture and nature

the dialogue between architecture and nature can be undertaken with strategies similar to those explained in the previous section, by contrast or by imitation of the built project. But it is also possible to define the architectural space with trees, shrubs, rocks, and water features that act as visual limits for the space. It is in the interaction of these natural spaces with more artificial ones where a field of architectural perceptual experiences emerges, leading to many valuable works.

Thus we find natural pergolas and canopies formed by vegetation, hedges that define walls, tree trunks that suggest columns, or pools that convey freshness, delineate barriers, and incorporate reflections of the surroundings. All of this joins together, like a garden or nearby orchard, or like a distant landscape visible through a picture window.

Thumbnail sketch in ink showing Fallingwater in Pennsylvania, by Frank Lloyd Wright.

EAMES STUDIO-HOUSE, BY CHARLES EAMES

This residence in California, belonging to the architect himself, is based on a very light and diaphanous metallic structure that opens and connects the interior and the exterior spaces, with the intention of integrating the house into a surrounding of graceful eucalyptus trees. The interior spaces are very high, the structural elements very slender, and the walls almost transparent, but without reaching the extremes of other residences in which the walls are of glass without woodwork. Here, the subdivision of the different windows allows for climatic control of the interior and makes the space comfortable to be in.

Eames studio-house, California, by Charles Eames.

Schematic thumbnail sketch in graphite pencil showing the building.

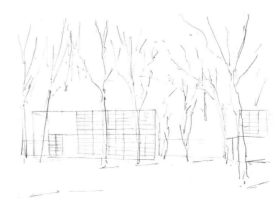

1

1. First the layout is drawn in pencil, with special attention to the surrounding vegetation.

2

This thumbnail sketch uses pencil in combination with a graphite stick in order to represent both the fine metallic outlines of the house as well as the branches of the trees and their leaves and, at the same time, the masses of foliage and the shadows. Above all, it conveys the sensation of being surrounded by a forest, a quality which, were it suggested in ink, would require very laborious shading throughout the drawing, and much more time. The process is the same as in the previous examples, but with a more expressive treatment of the eucalyptus leaves, created by using graphite stick strokes to produce tones of descending value, suggesting the knife-shaped leaves of the trees.

2. The different planes and planting masses are shaded.

3. Finally, the architectural structure is defined and the tree shapes suggested with pencil.

3

The use of the Archi-tectural drawing

"THE MOMENT OF TRUTH ARRIVES WHEN YOU MUST CONFRONT YOURSELF AND DRAW THE FIRST LINE OR THE FIRST BRUSHSTROKE IF YOU ARE AN ARTIST. THERE IS A POINT WHEN YOU MUST DECIDE, TAKE A DIRECTION. IT IS WHEN THE SHAPE OF THE BUILDING EMERGES."
Frank Gehry. Interview.

by Way

ÁLVARO SIZA.
IDEA SKETCH IN INK OF BORGES & IRMÃO BANK,
VILA DO CONDE, PORTUGAL

# of a summary.

Recognizing the architectural

drawing as the graphic

language of architecture, and having seen the basic principles of the alphabet, vocabulary, orthography, and grammar unique to architectural drawing, which correspond to the lines, shading, textures, dimensioned sketches, idea sketches, and thumbnail sketches, it is time to apply the language in order to begin expressing ourselves in this discipline. The process involves the synthesis of diverse examples of freehand drawings, essential in common practice.

We begin with a layout sketch of an existing work, with the dimensioned sketch playing the principal role. Then we continue with a first development of an unbuilt project that takes the work of other designers as a model or cultural reference, and the idea sketch becomes an indispensable tool. Finally, we conclude with graphic impressions in the form of a thumbnail sketch from a trip to Berlin.

Learning
from a master

In order to gather the lessons explained in this book and illustrate the common practice of architectural drawing in the form of the dimensioned sketch, we will concentrate on one of the most frequent examples, the survey of a building.

AN EMBLEMATIC CONSTRUCTION

The subject is the German Pavilion of Ludwig Mies van der Rohe, designed for the Universal Exposition of 1929 in Barcelona, Spain. At the close of the Exposition, the structure was demolished, as was traditional for these events. In 1984, thanks to public organizations and various entities, among them the Colegio Oficial de Arquitectos de Catalunya (Official college of Catalan architects) and the Escuela Técnica Superior de Arquitectura de Barcelona, and due to its enormous architectural significance, it was reconstructed on the original site. The great architectural value of this building lies in the fact that it constitutes one of the fundamental examples of the Modern Movement in architecture, and it exhibits a perfect synthesis of the architectural postulates of its designer, one of the great masters of this discipline.

Views from the exterior of the German Pavilion in Barcelona, Spain, by Mies van der Rohe.

The work, in a strict sense, is characterized by being based entirely on a grid over which is constructed an elevated platform where the different elements that compose it are located. Only two areas are covered, specifically with a lamina or flat floor structure. Beneath them are spaces organized and divided by smooth walls, also modulated, that extend toward the exterior.

These walls define passages and separate spaces. A remarkable feature of the walls is the way in which they surround two pools, one completely exterior and the other in an uncovered interior. Both reflections on the pools and the noble materials used in the construction (chrome-plated steel, marble, onyx, etc.) give the place a unique character.

1. First, a layout is drawn in pencil showing the plan and the modulation of the pavement.

2. Then the sketch of the plan is created on the base of the pavement, and the roofs and structural elements are added to it.

3. Finally, the sketch is completed with the partitions and vertical walls, the woodwork, and their measurements.

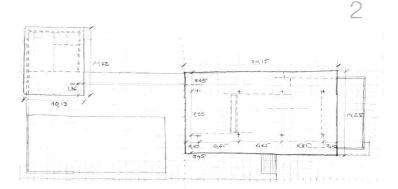

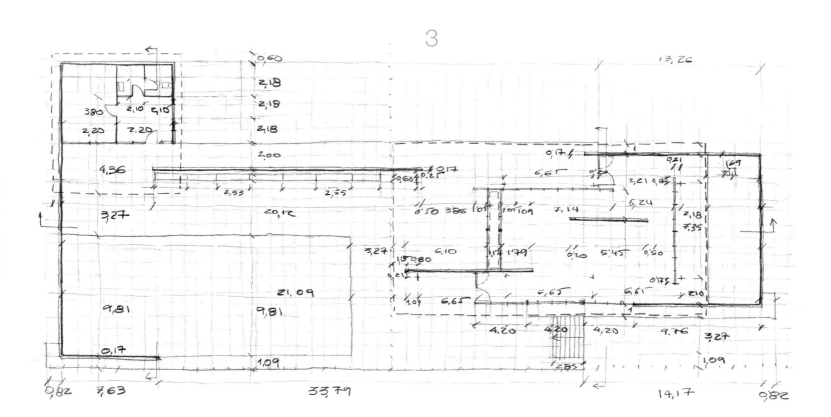

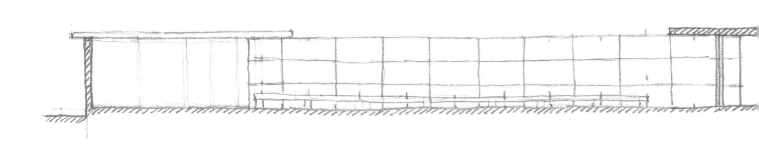

THE PROCESS

To begin the sketches, we have drawn guide lines over a base grid which, once measured, represents paving stones that are 1.09 m (3½ ft) square and stones in the vertical walls (except for the onyx) that are 1.03 by 2.18 m (3⅓ ft by 7 ft).

The plan is gradually defined at different stages of detail, beginning with the guide line of the pavement and continuing with the structure and the roofs. Once that is completed, we define all the elements that compose the plan: the walls, partitions, woodwork, etc. We then mark the contour lines on the plan as needed, measuring and using the underlying grid in order to abbreviate the dimensions.

Since the articulation of the building allows us to transfer the joints easily, using the same strategy we then draw the elevations and sections on separate sheets of paper. The cutting planes must be studied carefully in order to select what conveys the most information, thus avoiding numerous unnecessary or repetitive representations. Measuring is difficult because the joints of the pavement do not strictly correspond to the wall joints, and therefore many partial measurements must be taken.

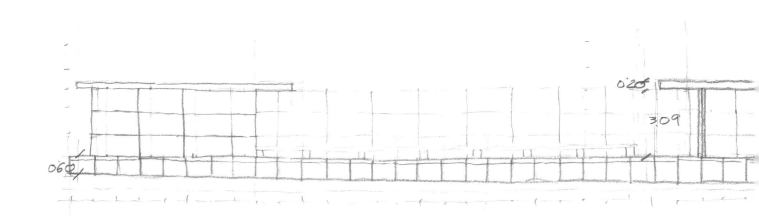

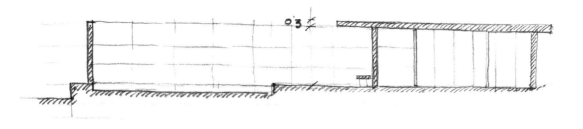

Pencil idea sketch of the transverse section as indicated on the plan shown on page 169. The cutting planes are chosen to provide the most information possible.

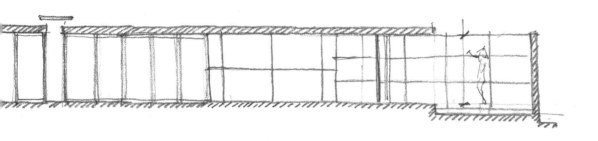

Pencil sketch of the longitudinal section indicated on the plan.

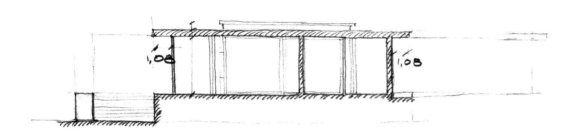

Pencil sketch of the transverse section shown on the plan. More than one section is virtually mandatory in studying a whole building.

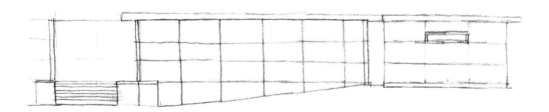

Pencil sketch of the side elevation of the building.

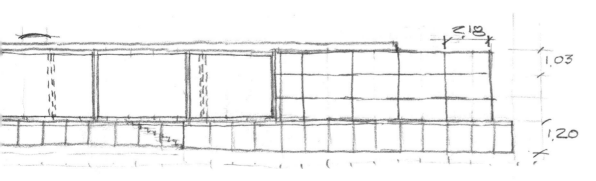

Pencil sketch of the front elevation of the building.

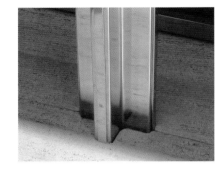

Image of the column in the Pavilion, whose reconstruction is the work of I. de Sola-Morales, C. Cirici, and F. Ramos.

IDEA SKETCHES OF DETAILS
AND COMPLEMENTS: COLUMNS AND FURNISHINGS

The precious and meticulous work of Mies Van der Rohe for this project led him to design a metallic column with a very unusual base, a work of art in which supporting elements like the metallic cover combine with ornamental characteristics like the chrome paneling. The expressionistic quality of the column compelled us to devote a detail sketch to it because it has become the symbol of the Pavilion, and it also serves to illustrate this sketch in greater detail. Given the flowing composition of the space, based on vertical and horizontal partitions that slide past each other, it is not possible to describe the building entirely with a perspective drawing. Therefore, it is necessary to use an isometric projection of the ensemble to comfortably express how all the elements that compose it are articulated.

A series of furnishings that Mies designed specifically for this building, the Barcelona chair and stool, complete the project. These have become worldwide icons of modernity. We have drawn some sketches of the chair; although the subject is more akin to interior design, it also relates to the architect's task of defining all the elements in a project, including the furnishings, especially if these are not prefabricated.

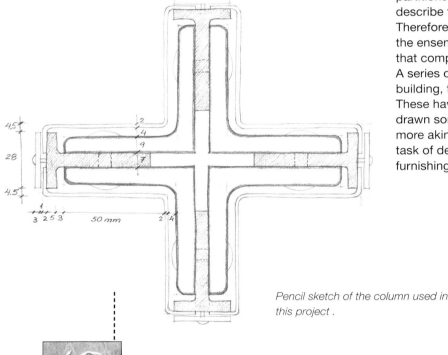

Pencil sketch of the column used in this project .

Sculpture, copy of the original, over one of the pools. It has become a visual reference for the Pavilion.

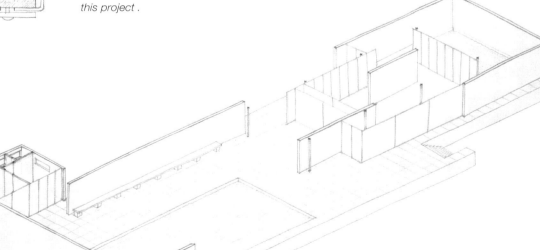

Isometric projection in pencil of the plan of the Pavilion, shown without the roof. This representation gives us a better understanding of the ensemble.

Barcelona chairs, designed by the architect for this project.

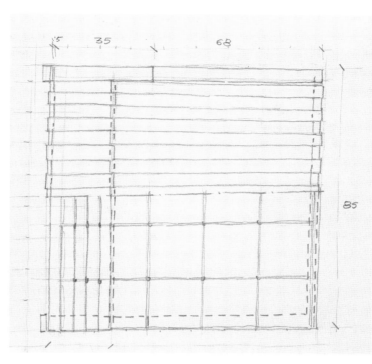

Pencil dimensioned sketch showing the design for the Barcelona chair describing both its structure and its upholstery.

Pencil sketch showing front, rear, and side elevations of the chair with numerous dimensions to define its curvatures.

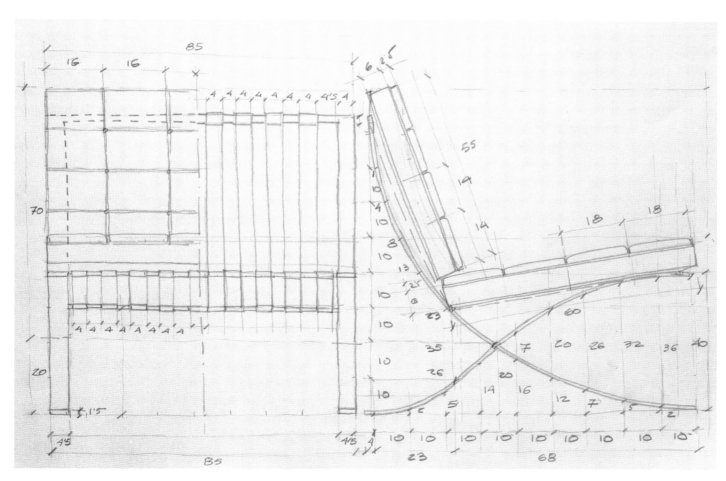

the idea sketch. Proposals
based on an idea

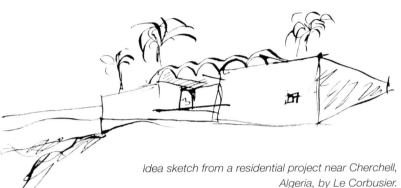

Idea sketch from a residential project near Cherchell, Algeria, by Le Corbusier.

In this section, the work of an architecture and design professional is illustrated at the phase most likely to generate different proposals or idea sketches—that is, in creating a project. It seemed appropriate to us to develop this project with the work of other architects as a model or cultural reference.

A STRUCTURAL TYPOLOGY AS AN EXAMPLE

We have concentrated here on the study of a particular construction system, which uses the Catalan vault that various well-known architects have adopted around the globe. The success of this structure lies in its economy and its coherence, as well in the quality of the resulting spaces. This structural typology was used previously on various occasions by Le Corbusier in France, specifically in the house in La Celle-Saint Cloud, near Paris, which dates from 1935; in the project for an agricultural residence in Cherchell (in what is now Algeria), from 1945; in the projects for apartments in Sainte Baume, from 1948; in Cap Martin, France, from 1949; in the Fueter House, Switzerland, of 1950; in the Jaoul House, near Paris, from 1952; and in the Sarabhai Residence in Ahmedabad, India, of 1955.

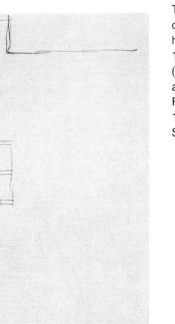

Pencil diagram showing the distribution of the vaults and of the third-floor of the residence by Le Corbusier.

Idea sketch in pencil of the plan and a section showing the Fueter House in Switzerland, by Le Corbusier. One of many examples where the Catalan vault is used.

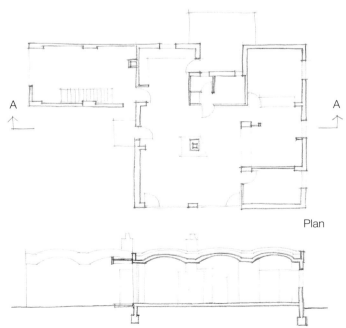

Plan

Section AA

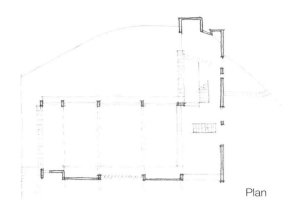

Plan

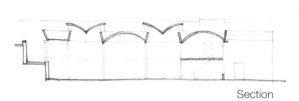

Section

Schematic idea sketch in pencil of the third floor and of section showing the studio of Joan Miró, Palma de Mallorca, Spain, by Josep Lluis Sert.

Schematic idea sketch in pencil showing the plans and elevations of commercial buildings, Tumaco, Colombia, by Josep Lluis Sert.

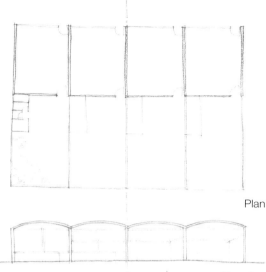

Plan

Elevation

In addition, some of his followers and disciples, among them Josep Lluis Sert, incorporated these vaults into low-cost housing projects for Colombia, Peru, Cuba, and the United States between 1939 and1953; and in the studio in Palma de Mallorca for the painter Joan Miró in 1955.

The Spanish architect Bonet Castellana, after working in the studio of Le Corbusier, used the vault in a group of houses in Martinez, Argentina, in 1940, and in the Berlingieri House in Punta Ballena in 1947. In Spain, significant examples by Bonet Castellana include the country house, La Ricarda, in

El Prat de Llobregat, Barcelona, in 1949; the Cruylles House, in Aiguablava, Girona, in 1967; the Raventos House in Calella de Palafrugell, Girona, in 1973; and the Atamaria Apartments, Murcia, in 1973. Gaudí, Guastavino, Eladio Dieste, and others also used the Catalan vault. We have drawn schematic idea sketches of some of these residences, illustrative of their distribution in plan, as well as an elevation and section, where the presence of the vaults is clearly displayed.

Schematic idea sketch in pencil showing the plan and a section of houses, Martinez, Argentina, by Antonio Bonet Castellana.

Schematic idea sketch in pencil showing the plan and a section of the country house, La Ricarda, El Prat de Llobregat, Spain, by Antonio Bonet Castellana.

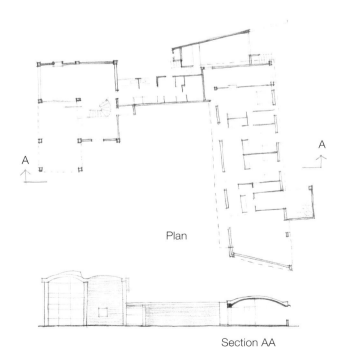

Plan

A

A

Section AA

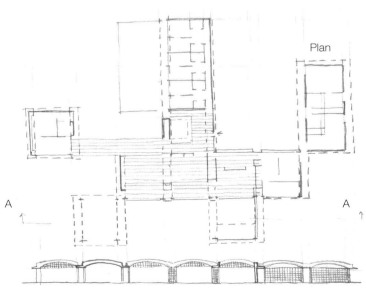

Plan

A

A

Section AA

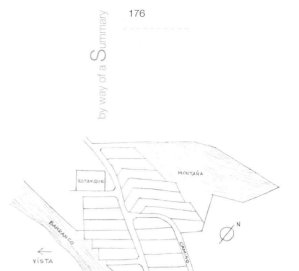

Diagram of the situation and surroundings of the land, showing where it lies relative to the island of Tenerife.

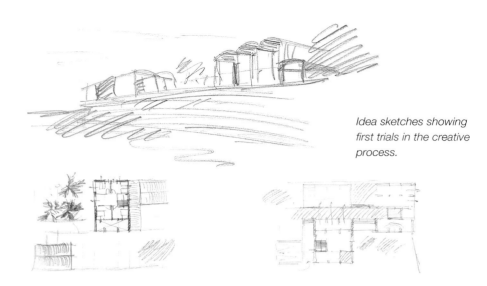

Idea sketches showing first trials in the creative process.

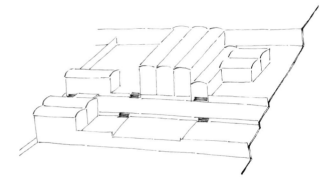

Axonometric schematic idea sketch in ink of the project's two structures, describing their siting on the terrain.

THE IDEA SKETCH OF A PROJECT

With the Catalan vault as a construction system and a system of spatial design, we consider the idea sketches for a residential project on an agricultural site in Tenerife, in the Canary Islands, Spain. More specifically, it is a residence on a plantation for bananas and other crops in La Punta, Candelaria, on the south side of the island, chosen for its unusual geology and climate.

Our project finds inspiration in all the references described above, presenting a residence composed of two isolated structures on a terraced site surrounded by protective stone walls. One structure constitutes the actual residence, occupying two floors; the other is a loggia on one floor. The two are connected by a passage or pergola along which a stream of water passes. The stream flows from the general reservoir of the plantation and continues its course to a pond, a small canal, and a swimming pool, contributing climate control and comfort to its surroundings.

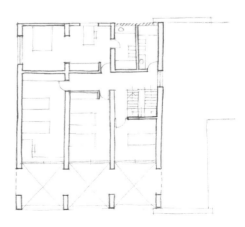

Schematic idea sketch in pencil of the third floor of the residence.

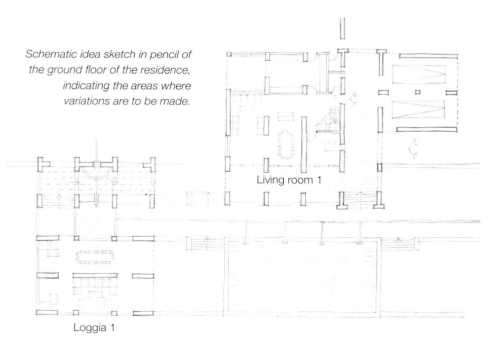

Schematic idea sketch in pencil of the ground floor of the residence, indicating the areas where variations are to be made.

Living room 1

Loggia 1

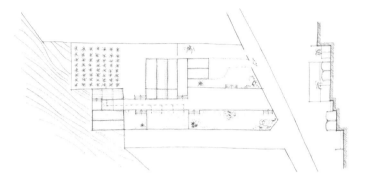

Schematic idea sketch in pencil of the location and distribution of the project on the terrain and section describing the different existing and newly created levels.

In order to suggest depth, the elevations are represented in varying degrees of detail, according to whether the planes are nearer or farther away. The sense of depth is also communicated by reducing the contrast, in the same way.

IDEA SKETCHES OF THE EXTERIOR

The layout of the residence, based on a series of corridors covered by ceramic or concrete vaults, presents a very ordered structure of parallel spaces, more or less connected depending on the thickness and extension of the supporting walls.
As for the terraced section of the site and the introduction of the building to it, a selection of elevations and sections illustrate the integration of the building into its surroundings, as well as the expressiveness of the roofs and the transparency of the setting.

Idea sketch in ink of the side elevation oriented toward the ravine.

Idea sketch in ink of the front elevation where the interaction between light and shadow is studied, together with the vegetation and the different textures.

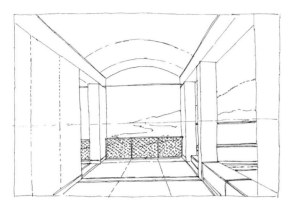

Idea sketch in felt-tip pen, in line only, of the interior area of loggia 1 with the initial proposal for the plan.

Idea sketch in felt-tip pen, with some textures, showing the same view of loggia 2 in a variation of the plan.

Idea sketch in felt-tip pen, with textures and shadows from the same exterior view, of loggia 1, the initial proposal for the plan.

IDEA SKETCHES OF THE INTERIOR

By playing with the configuration of the walls, various spaces can be created—more or less closed, linear, or open in different directions. These proposals are illustrated through idea sketches. In this case, two settings are considered with some variations.

The first is the loggia or porch, whose appearance changes by altering the extension of the walls and columns that support the vaults. In order to visualize these alternatives and graphically test the result that can be obtained with the changes, several quick idea sketches have been drawn in felt-tip pen, displaying different degrees of finish in the line, texture, shadows, and atmosphere.

Idea sketch in felt-tip pen, with textures, from the exterior view of loggia 2, in a variation of the plan.

Variation in the plan showing the area of the loggia where the walls are reduced in comparison to the first proposal.

Loggia 2

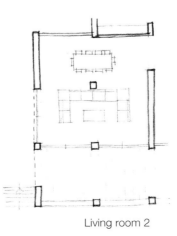

Living room 2

Variation in the plan showing the living-room area of the residence where the walls are reduced in comparison to the first proposal.

Idea sketch in pencil, with textures and shadows, showing the view from an interior point of living room 1, with broad walls. The walls have the texture of brick and the vault the texture of plaster.

The living room of the residence is the subject of another series of graphic variations and trials. It is essential to carry out these trials before making a final decision about the project.

The various proposals for alterations are presented in a series of idea sketches that offer a preview of the final appearance of the space, depending on the size of the walls and columns and the nature of the construction materials or finishes used for the vertical supports and vaults. The first proposal, as in the previous case, causes the spaces and the exterior views to open and expand as the walls diminish in size. The space, as shown on the following page, becomes more transparent and luminous.

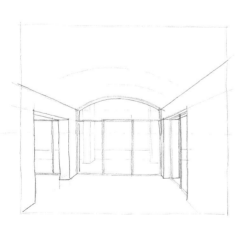

As the first step in the idea sketch, we create a layout with pencil lines to define the spatial volume.

Idea sketch in pencil, with textures and shadows, showing the same view of living room 1 with different materials: stone for the walls and wood for the vault.

Idea sketch in pencil with textures and shadows showing the view from another interior point in living room 2, but with reduced walls. The textures are brick for the walls and concrete for the vault.

The materials play a decisive role in the visual sensations that are expressed. If the vault is white, greater luminosity is achieved. If, on the other hand, a warmer ambiance is desired, with less luminosity, the vault may be covered in wood, for example. The same applies to the effect produced when using materials like brick or stone for the walls or columns.
This project has been presented with a few basic elements combined in a couple of variations. These examples seem sufficient to communicate the proposed idea. Needless to say, numerous possibilities exist, especially if more materials are introduced into this game of previsualization.

Idea sketch in pencil with textures and shadows showing the same view, but with different materials: plaster on the walls and a layer of brick on the vault.

Layout in pencil drawn before the idea sketch.

The only recommended tools are a white pencil for light and highlights and a black pencil for the rest, so that the image of the photograph is visible beneath the strokes.

Photomontage over the image in black and white, printed on drawing paper, showing a view of the loggia with the landscape in the background. The achromatic range of grays of charcoal pencils and chalk blends easily with the tones of the photograph.

PHOTOMONTAGE

Proposals can also be presented to test the visual result of situating ourselves at a point in the building being studied, with the building set in its real surroundings.

In order to avoid representing the surroundings, some simple idea sketch—photomontages are created by drawing with black and white pencils over photocopies of images of the location that have been printed on drawing paper. Thus, the exceptional views of the location, which should be emphasized and considered one of the key themes of the project, can easily be worked on to evaluate the result of the proposals, with minimal possibility of error.

In all these cases, the drawing and the concept form a whole, and technique should matter the least. However, in order to achieve this level of expertise, one must be familiar with the most common and versatile techniques, managing and mastering them completely. Only then can the ideas that spring from the mind be expressed and constructed.

nowadays, a trip to Berlin offers much to anyone interested in architecture. The center of this city, since the demolition of the historic wall that divided it, has experienced a spectacular urban transformation, created by major contemporary architects. For this reason, when considering an example of common practice among professionals in which the architectural drawing is employed in the form of a thumbnail sketch, we thought a trip to Berlin seemed an appropriate model.

Berlin.
Sketches from a trip

ACCOUNT OF THE VISIT

For four days, Magali Delgado and Ernest Redondo visited the most typical parts of the city, as well as many of the recent buildings, producing various drawings, some quick, others more elaborate. In each drawing, we tried to emphasize one of the architectural values of the building, whether that was its uniqueness, its originality, its construction technology, its urban scale, its integration with the surroundings or with another existing building, and so on.

Thumbnail sketch of the Brandenburg Gate. A very thick graphite lead was used in order to darken the scene because it was a rainy day.

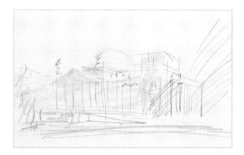

Thumbnail sketch in pencil of Berlin Philharmonic Hall. The vegetation was shaded, with the buildings behind highlighted by backlighting.

Rapid thumbnail sketch of the same building.

Rapid thumbnail sketch of the Reichstag, the German parliament.

A drawing can replace a photograph of a building; the photograph does not easily capture the essence of the place, unlike the more elaborate thumbnail drawing. The drawing requires more time for completion, so its creator becomes fully immersed in the ambiance.

The technique employed was always graphite pencil on a drawing pad measuring 8 1/2 by 11 inches. The time devoted to each drawing varied from five minutes for the quickest to half an hour for others. Most were executed from a standing position. First, we visited the outskirts of the Tiergarten Park and the Brandenburg Gate, master plan by Josef P. Kleihues; the Reichstag, or parliament, whose restoration has been the work of Norman Foster; and the landmark Berlin Philharmonic Hall of Hans Scharoun.

Thumbnail sketch in pencil of the Reichstag. The depth of the scene is reinforced by the overlap and gradation of planes of varying luminosity.

THE SECOND DAY

After entering the glass cupola of the Reichstag, whose lightness and technology are astonishing, we spent the following days visiting other places of interest, taking advantage of sunny moments in the cold Berlin spring. First, we went to the neighborhood of the new embassies, on the outskirts of the Klingelhofer Strasse, and then continued toward Potsdamer Platz, once again the vital center of the city.

On our first stop, we worked on final drawings of the Nordic embassies designed by a team of several architects: Berger & Parkkinen, VIVA Arkkitehtuuri, and others. Then we made some thumbnail sketches of the Sony Center by Helmut Jahn of Murphy/Jahn and of the two slender office buildings, one by Hans Kollhoff and the other by Renzo Piano, visual milestones in the landscape of Berlin's new center.

Rapid thumbnail sketch in pencil of the Nordic embassies ensemble.

Thumbnail sketch of the same headquarters; sketching the vanishing lines helps suggest the wood and glass envelope of the buildings.

Rapid thumbnail sketch of Potsdamer Platz.

Thumbnail sketch of the unique buildings on Potsdamer Platz. The vertical orientation of the drawing reinforces the urban scale.

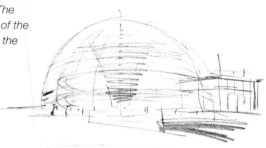

Rapid thumbnail sketch of the cupola of the Reichstag.

Thumbnail sketch in pencil of the glass roof of the Reichstag. A thick graphite lead is used again in order to darken part of the scene, leaving the highlights of the glass in white.

Thumbnail sketch in pencil of the central headquarters of the CDU party. This drawing highlights the transparency of the glass canopy and the interior building.

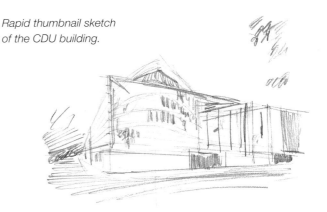

Rapid thumbnail sketch of the CDU building.

THIRD AND FOURTH DAYS

On the following days, we revisited the same places and took notes on the building that houses the central headquarters of the CDU (Christian Democratic Union political party), the work of Petzinka, Pink, and Partner, near the embassies. This interpretation of the building is unusual: it is shown from the corner, where transparencies and formal contrasts allow the interaction of urban setting with the interior space. Then we continued our walk along the Reichpietsch Ufer and Schelling Strasse, drawing buildings whose urban character expresses the grand scale of the project, by Renzo Piano and Rafael Moneo. After returning to Pariser Platz and the Brandenburg Gate, we prepared a thumbnail sketch of the headquarters of the D. G. Bank by Frank O. Gehry. We briefly entered the interior of this structure, whose facade folds over itself in a clear allusion and reinterpretation of the crowded facades of traditional houses along the avenues of Berlin.

Thumbnail sketch of the office buildings on the streets that converge at Potsdamer Platz, showing the urban appearance of the setting from a somewhat forced point of view.

Rapid thumbnail sketch of the office buildings.

Rapid thumbnail sketch of the D. G. Bank building.

Thumbnail sketch in pencil of the D. G. Bank building in which we managed to represent all the levels and floors, as well as the articulation of the facade. This drawing took more time than usual.

Our last stop was the obligatory visit to the Jewish Museum, work of Daniel Libeskind, on Lindenstrasse. The closed structure, its fractured composition, and the skin of the facade suggest the drama of the events to which the building is dedicated.

The continual transformation of this city surely warrants another visit in a few years, to stroll along its avenues observing the brilliant new buildings that will call for new drawings. These keep the memory alive in our minds, while at the same time, with their creation, we better understand and learn about architecture.

Rapid thumbnail sketch of the Jewish Museum.

Thumbnail sketch of the Jewish Museum emphasizing the treatment and appearance of the metallic facade in contrast with the planting.

A

Angle of Vision. Angle formed by the visual lines drawn from the observer to the most extreme edges of the view.

Axonometric. System of projection that creates a single view of an architectural volume from an exterior point by means of its projection in one direction so that the projecting lines are parallel to each other.

Axonometric projection. Drawing convention involving the perpendicular projection of the subject against a plane of projection.

C

Cast shadow. Area hidden from the light source by the shadowed part of an object blocking another that is found in the same path of the light source.

Center of vision (C.O.V.). Perpendicular projection on the horizon line of the point of view. The distance between the point of view and the center of vision defines the central axis of vision.

Chiaroscuro. Graphic technique that represents the volume of a form by means of graduated tones of light and shadow.

Composition. Organizational structure of a drawing and its different elements as they appear together on the paper.

Contour drawing. Variant of orthographic projection in which any object is projected perpendicularly over a single horizontal plane of projection. Its height is defined by numeric values, contour lines, or flat sections of the plane at a particular height.

D

Dimensions. Numbers that indicate the real measurements of any architectural element.

Drawing plane (D.P.). Plane of projection in one-point perspective, product of the intersection of the visual pyramid with the vertical plane. Also called picture plane, which refers to the canvas or surface that is employed in drawing or painting.

E

Elevation. Perpendicular view of the outside of a building in orthographic projection. Referred to as principal (or main) side, or according to its orientation (north, south, east, west).

Elevation or section oblique. Axonometric projection in which the elevation or section is parallel to the plane of projection. The remaining edges extend from them at parallel angles.

Edge. Line or contour that defines the border of a plane or the meeting of two planes.

G

Gradation. Sequence of contiguous tones that range from a light value to a darker one in a continuous or regulated manner.

Gradient. Scale or measured variation of tonal values (or colors) along a given surface.

Graphic conventions. Standards used to unify the graphic language of architecture so that it can be understood by all.

Graphic scale. Guide on a drawing that indicates the equivalent to some element or dimension of the subject and thus serves as the basis for the proportions of the drawing.

Graphic symbols. Informational icons, sometimes without a proportional scale, that describe schematically particular technical groups of furnishings, surroundings, or different instructions.

Hardness of lead. In a graphite pencil, the quantity of clay, which produces greater solidity and diminishes the intensity of the tone.

Hatching. Collection of superimposed strokes or dots, or both, used to produce tonal shading with instruments that produce linear marks.

Highlights. Points or areas of maximum illumination in a scene, corresponding to the brightest white value on the tonal scale.

Horizon line (H.L.). Line that forms the intersection between the drawing plane and the horizon plane at eye level of the observer.

Hue. Quality of a color that characterizes it and distinguishes it from other colors in a chromatic model.

L

Labeling. Collection of words that describe the material qualities, instructions for installation, and type of projection or other data of interest in an architectural drawing.

Layout. Framework of simple geometric forms that serves to proportion a drawing.

Layout line. Lightly drawn line used to lay out the contours of a form.

Lighting scheme. Collection of light sources, shadows, and reflective surfaces that compose a scene.

Luminosity or value. Quality of a color that defines the quantity of light or of black and white in its composition.

M
Measuring line (M.L.). Line that, when the drawing plane coincides with one of the edges of the model, presents a projection of identical size. Any measurement can be defined along this edge.

O
Oblique or two-point perspective. System of representation in which neither of the two edges of the grid of the subject are parallel with the drawing plane, requiring two vanishing points on the horizon where parallel lines converge.

One-point (frontal) perspective. System of representation based on the principle that all elements are projected onto a plane in a convergent way, by means of visual rays that emerge from one point and end at each one of its vertices, the result being a pyramid.

Orthogonal. Perpendicular to a plane or line.

Orthographic projection. System based on the representation of a form by means of diverse projections over planes perpendicular to each other with simultaneous points of view from the infinite.

P
Paper grain. Degree of roughness in the texture of drawing paper.

Plan. Orthogonal projection resulting from cutting a building along a particular horizontal plane.

Plan oblique. Axonometric projection in which the plan is parallel to the plane of projection. The remaining edges extend from it at parallel angles.

Point of view (P.V.) or station point. Center of projection, where the observer is located.

S
Saturation. Quality of a color that defines its purity with respect to one of the pigments or pure components of its composition.

Section. Orthogonal projection resulting from cutting an element on a particular vertical plane.

Shade. Variance in the illumination of a surface when an element has one part exposed to the light and another part hidden from the light.

Shading. Tonal variation in one part of the drawing that indicates degrees of shade or shadow of a model in order to express its volume.

Sources of light. Elements that emit light in a real or pictorial scene.

Station point. *See* Point of view.

Survey. Collection of plans, elevations, and sections of a building, produced to scale or annotated.

Systems of representation. Graphic conventions that allow all architectural elements to be represented on paper.

T
Texture. Surface quality of a material. In architectural drawing, the application of shading in order to convey the surface qualities of a material and indicate its nature.

Tonal scale. Scale of graduated values ranging from black to white in an achromatic drawing. Also called value scale.

Value. Lightness or darkness of a color. If achromatic, it defines the degree of black in it.

Two-point perspective. *See* Oblique perspective.

V
Value. *See* Luminosity.

Vanishing point (V.P.). Point toward which a bundle of straight parallel lines converge in linear perspective.

View. Projection of an architectural form in some systems of representation equivalent to the appearance of the projection from a particular place.

bibliography

• Arnheim, Rudolf. *Art and Visual Perception.* 2nd rev. ed. Berkeley: University of California, Press, 1974.

• Ching, Frank D. K. *Architectural Graphics.* 4th ed. Hoboken, N.J.: John Wiley & Sons, 2002.

• Laseau, Paul. *Freehand Sketching: An Introduction.* New York: W. W. Norton & Company, 2003.

• Mayer, Ralph, and Steven Sheehan. *The Artists Handbook of Materials and Techniques.* 5th ed. New York: Penguin, 1991.

• Porter, Tom, and Sue Goodman. *Manual of Graphic Techniques for Architects, Graphic Designers and Artists.* London: Architectural Press, 1988.

• Vagnetti, Luigi. *Il lenguaggio grafico dell'architetto.* Genoa: Editorial Vitale e Ghianda, 1965.

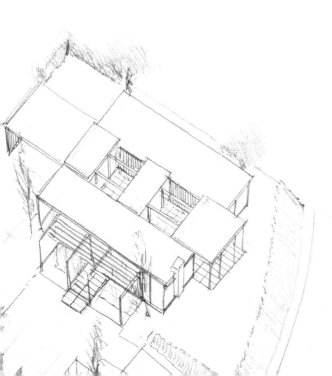

Acknowledgments

To our parents. And our loved ones for their encouragement and for the free time that we stole from them.

To Charlie Conesa for the generous contribution of his drawings to the book.

To our colleagues at the University; Lluis Villanueva, for his consideration in reviewing the texts and advising us on the descriptive geometry sections, and to Javier Monedero, Margarita Galceran, Manolo Luque, and Isabel Ruiz.

To the Elsa Peretti Foundation for facilitating the preparation of drawings in Sant Marti Vell (Girona).

The stationery store at the Escola Técnica Superior d'Arquitectura de Barcelona for providing us with graphic material to be photographed.

The library of the Pabellón de la República at the University of Barcelona for giving us the opportunity to develop one of our themes there.

The following architects, publishers, architecture studios, and foundations for their kindness in allowing reproduction of their drawings or for their collaboration: Alvaro Siza; Alvar Aalto Foundation; Birkhäuser Verlag (for the drawings by Le Corbusier published in Le Corbusier 1910–65); Arxiu Coderch; Emili Donato; El Croquis magazine; Enric Miralles Benedetta Tagliabue EMBT Arquitectes Associats, S.L. and collaborators; Fondation Le Corbuser; Gustavo Gili, Publisher; Serbal Editions; Felix Solaguren-Beascoa (for the drawings by Arne Jacobsen); Williams & Tsien; Peter Zumthor.

And for the American edition, the assistance of Paul Laseau and German Tadeo Cruz, and Santiago Castán Gómez, who contributed their knowledge to the translation by Maria Fleming Alvarez.

Index